CW01011204

SOUTH AFRICA'S
greatest golf destinations

STRUIK
TRAVEL &
HERITAGE

SOUTH AFRICA'S
greatest golf destinations

JAMIE THOM with **STUART McLEAN**

Contents

1. Atlantic Beach
2. Milnerton
3. Royal Cape
4. Steenberg
5. Clovelly
6. Erinvale
7. Arabella
8. Hermanus
9. Pearl Valley
10. De Zalze
11. Stellenbosch
12. Pinnacle Point
13. Oubaai
14. The Links at Fancourt
15. Fancourt Montagu
16. Fancourt Outeniqua
17. George
18. Simola
19. Pezula
20. Goose Valley
21. St Francis Links
22. Humewood
23. Royal Port Alfred
24. Fish River Sun
25. East London
26. Wild Coast Sun
27. San Lameer
28. Southbroom
29. Umdoni Park
30. Selborne
31. Durban Country Club
32. Beachwood
33. Zimbali
34. Prince's Grant
35. Cotswold Downs
36. Victoria Country Club
37. Champagne Sports
38. Euphoria
39. Hans Merensky
40. Leopard Creek
41. Zebula Country Club
42. Elements
43. Lost City
44. Gary Player Country Club
45. Sishen
46. Pretoria Country Club
47. Silver Lakes
48. Maccauvlei
49. Pecanwood
50. Gardener Ross
51. Blair Atholl
52. Country Club Johannesburg: Woodmead & Rocklands
53. River Club
54. Royal Johannesburg & Kensington: East & West
55. Glendower
56. Ebotse

Foreword

There are many of us who share the sentiments of the late Ben Hogan, expressed at a dinner honouring all the legends of golf more than a decade ago. In closing his talk, he said, 'I love this game,' and wiping away a tear, he added, 'I really, really love this game.'

Personally, I would add that I really, really love golf design and all its great courses. I admire the famous old designers from Colt, Alison and Mackenzie to Ross and Tillinghast, and locally, a lovely old Englishman who settled at Scottburgh in KwaZulu-Natal, Bob Grimsdell, who did good work throughout South Africa. But I think the modern designers are just as talented and are producing outstanding golf courses, especially considering the land available. I am a little concerned, though, about where golf design is going, with demands for more spectacular and more 'signature' holes – a pet hate of mine. We need to bring back the 'golf' into golf design and create classic courses with balance and variety.

I am blessed to have the opportunity to be involved in many new courses and to upgrade some of the old courses, but golf design is not

about me, it is about a team. Translating the design from what is on paper and then putting it in the ground – that is the tough part and requires team effort. From my design assistant, Louis van der Walt, to the shapers on the excavators and bulldozers and the people who do the raking and planting, I have a truly talented and dedicated team of professionals. We have had so much fun working in the mountains of Zimbabwe's Leopard Rock and the spectacular cliffs at Pinnacle Point, even moving huge waste dumps at Ebotse. We all share the same love for the environment – the fauna and flora.

Jamie Thom and Stuart McLean share that love and passion for golf and are the ultimate professionals. Jamie has captured all those sentiments, moods and feelings through his lens and, with Stuart, has produced a very special book. Jamie's background in wildlife photography instilled in him an understanding of natural light and what it is to be patient, to wait for a shot. Many people believe that you can just fly in and out of a golf course to get the photographs and do not appreciate the planning, effort and waiting that is involved to get the desired results. Jamie's images, complemented by Stuart's concise and informative text, bring out the character of each course, from the lovely old gems to the splendour of the modern courses.

I am sure this book will inspire golfers to travel and play these courses. Most of all, I am hoping it will encourage overseas visitors to visit our beautiful country and enjoy all the world-class courses that make South Africa a truly magnificent golfing destination.

I have longed for a book of this nature so that I can proudly stand it alongside the many books on famous golf courses in other countries that line my bookshelves. For this I thank my friends Jamie and Stuart, whose book it is an honour and pleasure to recommend.

Peter Matkovich
Matkovich & Hayes Golf Estate Solutions

Introduction

Photographing golf courses combines my passion for the game of golf, for being outdoors and creative, and for golf courses themselves. I feel privileged to derive an income from doing something I love. Spending the amount of time I have on golf courses has enabled me to look beyond what most people see, and appreciate them on another level.

My first chance to see 'inside' a golf course was at Elements Private Golf Reserve near Bela-Bela in Limpopo. I was tasked with photographing the course from before ground was broken to the finished product. Every few months I made the two-hour drive to the Waterberg bushveld, and watching the course develop was fascinating. The engineering and technical side of it was complex – how greens are built in layers, the irrigation system and its wiring, managing the flow and storage of water. The creative aspect was also intriguing – watching golf course designer Peter Matkovich pace out the holes and plan each detail, such as what trees were going to be part of the design, where a bunker would go, the positioning of a tee box, the slope of a fairway and the shape of a green. Once you know what is involved in building a golf course and what is below ground level, you have a new appreciation of what is above the ground. The vision and imagination of a good course designer is a marvel; it is 'art and engineering in the ground'.

South Africa has a rich golfing history and a handful of courses that are more than a hundred years old. The first golf club formed in the country was in the Cape, around 1885, where members played on a course called Waterloo Green, which is now Royal Cape. Our first national championship was held in Kimberley in 1892 and our first Open Championship in Port Elizabeth in 1903. Golf courses have come a long way since those flat and simple layouts. Earthmoving machinery allows a bland piece of land to be shaped into just about anything. New methods of construction, modern irrigation systems and highly scientific horticultural practices, aided by big budgets and modern design styles, explain how the expansive courses of today have been achieved.

With my photographs I have tried to capture the character of each course and what defines it. I like to show the hole in the most beautiful way, but I also try to show it the way golfers would see it so that they can imagine themselves playing it.

With an extensive library of images, the thought of a book had been in the back of my mind when Random House Struik called to ask if I was interested in collaborating on a golf travel guide to South Africa. I presented my idea of what I wanted to produce and from both these concepts this book was born.

The travel aspect seemed appropriate because travelling in South Africa is one of the most satisfying aspects of my work. From Alicedale and Kathu to Port Edward and Phalaborwa, I have met wonderful people and been reminded of how extraordinary South Africa is. The beauty of our landscapes and the warmth of our people are ever-present. South Africa's diversity is reflected in our more than two hundred 18-hole golf courses. We have grand old courses, stunning natural links courses, parkland courses with towering trees lining the fairways, and dramatic courses built along ocean cliffs, among vineyards, high up in the mountains, in the bushveld and in game reserves. Bushveld courses are unique to South Africa and it is no surprise that many of our most highly rated courses are found in this category. In this book I have tried to illustrate this variety and showcase our top-ranked courses.

The final course photographed for this book was Sishen in the Northern Cape. I had been looking for a reason to go there and when it jumped up the Golf Digest rankings, I decided to make the six-hour trip from Johannesburg to Kathu. And I am glad I did. Sishen exemplifies what I love about golf courses – photography and travel. It is a magnificent course that plays among majestic camelthorn trees, and is possibly the prettiest I have ever photographed, an astounding gem in a little mining town that few people visit.

South Africa has many such places and I hope this book will grow the game of golf and promote our industry, as well as spread the message of what a fabulous golf destination this country is.

NOTES ON PHOTOGRAPHY

Photographing golf courses requires the right equipment, planning, time, patience and luck.

I have used a variety of camera gear, but have really fallen in love with my panoramic camera. Originally I shot 6x12cm film but the film I preferred using became difficult to source, which led me to buy digital equipment. I now use a medium format Leaf digital back on a Horseman panoramic camera, with 45mm, 65mm and 135mm lenses. Using this camera is like driving a Rolls Royce; it is a big, heavy camera but produces exceptional results.

Panoramic cameras really suit golf courses, which are largely wide scenes that need to be captured. Having a 'large' format means you need to fill up the image or else you get empty, or blank, areas. Any type of landscape photography requires pacing around and looking for the right combination of elements to compose the image and it is the same for golf courses except that the green and flag almost always forms the focal point of the image. Any form of elevation is also useful because it allows you to see more features of the course, such as bunkers and hazards.

Planning my shoots means being at the golf course when it is looking good. This is usually after it has had good rain and there is healthy grass growth. It is ideal if the course has been prepared for an event, but this still does not guarantee that I will get what I want.

The trump card is the weather. Few people understand the specific conditions required to achieve exceptional results. The holy grail of light for most photographers is clear light with no haze, which remains clear until the sun reaches the horizon. Blank blue skies are not ideal, as some cloud is required to add dimension. However, the number of those extraordinary days in a year could probably be counted on two hands. Usually I just have to make the best of what I have because I do not have two weeks for each shoot.

This is where patience plays its part. I need to be out there waiting for the clouds to part, waiting for golfers to move off the hole I am shooting, waiting for the sprinklers to switch off, or waiting for some shadows to move. And even then the window of opportunity is very short. There is no short cut and no software that can make it exceptional. I just have to be there … waiting and hoping.

Sishen in the Northern Cape is one of the most memorable and attractive golf courses in South Africa.

THE winelands

Whether it is playing golf alongside the Atlantic Ocean while the sun sets next to Table Mountain, sipping a glass of wine on a clubhouse terrace after playing 18 holes among the Stellenbosch vineyards, or watching whales in Walker Bay before a game at Hermanus, the Western Cape and its Winelands region have much to offer the golfer.

There is a broad range of golf courses to enjoy in a variety of different settings, from old-fashioned parkland venues – including South Africa's oldest golf club, Royal Cape, founded in 1885 – to the most modern resort and estate layouts designed by the likes of Jack Nicklaus, Gary Player and Peter Matkovich. The region includes golf in and about the Cape Peninsula, up the West Coast, in the scenic vineyards around Stellenbosch, Paarl and the Franschhoek valley, and further east from Cape Town, over the mountains, at the popular holiday resort of Hermanus.

Given the region's Mediterranean climate, dry in summer and wet in winter, golf is best enjoyed here from late September through to the end of May. While it can be windy during summer, the beauty of playing in the Cape is the chance golfers have to escape to some of the more sheltered courses in the area.

Pearl Valley

COURSE DESIGNER Jack Nicklaus
OPENED 2003

When Jack Nicklaus first inspected the Winelands site of what is today Pearl Valley Golf Estates, he was met by an assortment of wild animals placidly roaming the property. It was then a safari park. The animals have long since departed, to be replaced by one of the country's premier golf estates and a championship course that has already been host to two South African Opens.

Pearl Valley was a Malaysian development, but in 2007 ownership passed to Leisurecorp, a Dubai World company that invested substantially in the estate and the staging of the SA Open in 2007 and 2008. The clubhouse and course is the only one in South Africa managed by Troon Golf, the world's largest golf management company.

The estate lies close to Paarl, at the start of the wide Franschhoek valley that leads to the vineyards and quaint town of the same name – a magnet for tourists and locals with its wineries, restaurants and hostelries. The estate homes are lavish, in keeping with Pearl Valley's upmarket image. While the signature Nicklaus course is open to the public, visiting golfers pay a high price for one of the best conditioned layouts in the southern hemisphere.

This was Nicklaus's second South African design, and the routing and shaping reflect his creative qualities. Overlooked by mountains on either side, the estate is built on a flat piece of land, so he did not have much to work with in terms of inspiration. Nicklaus has succeeded in producing a visually pleasing layout where each hole is a separate entity. Water features, natural-looking mounding, rough grasses, indigenous vegetation and pine trees create a sense of golfing isolation among the houses.

Strategic and aesthetic bunkering from tee to green is a feature of Nicklaus designs, and Pearl Valley stands out as possibly the best bunkered layout in South Africa. The bunkers present constant challenges hole after hole, their sandy presence forcing golfers to take brave routes that can be disastrous.

Nicklaus designed Pearl Valley to be a true championship experience. Back tees can stretch the course to 6 801 metres, making it a natural SA Open venue. Ernie Els scored 64 in the final round of the 2008 Open, but before that tournament he had shot 77 three times, evidence of how difficult the course can be if you are not on your game.

Pearl Valley's par-three 4th (left) and par-four 16th (overleaf) show the course's superb conditioning and strategic bunkering.

De Zalze

COURSE DESIGNER Peter Matkovich
OPENED 2000

Wine and golf have always been inextricably linked at De Zalze, a relatively new golf estate on the outskirts of Stellenbosch. Since it opened in 2000, it has helped increase the growth of the university town. Vineyards are everywhere to be seen within and around the golf course, and the club originally shared premises with the award-winning Kleine Zalze wine estate before building its own clubhouse. Golfers used to sit on a patio under ancient shady oaks outside what is now Terroir restaurant, one of the top dining destinations in the Cape. Today you still walk past the winery buildings on your way from the 1st green to the 2nd tee.

De Zalze was developed by the Spier Group, and the Peter Matkovich golf course was originally known as Spier Country Club before crafting its own identity with the growth of the estate and opening of the clubhouse in 2003. In its first decade it has established itself as a premier golfing destination in the Cape, and in 2006 jointly hosted the World Amateur Team Championships with the neighbouring Stellenbosch Golf Club.

The narrow Blaauwklippen River, its banks lined by oak trees, is a natural feature of the course, running alongside five of the opening and closing holes. Matkovich used this stream to create a dramatic 18th hole, which is a shortish par four played from a high tee on a boulder next to the vineyards to a green on the other side of the water. Long hitters invariably go for glory here, while the more cautious have to be precise in avoiding a giant oak that hangs over the stream.

Other features on the course include a par five with two separate fairways sweeping around a large bunker, allowing different routes to the green; and tees placed in deep water on one of the estate's dams, for an exciting forced carry to the angled fairway on a short par four.

Stellenbosch airfield adjoins the estate, and there was a moment of drama a few years ago when a Harvard had to make an emergency landing on the 17th fairway. Fortunately, no one was injured, although a couple on a golf cart had a narrow escape when the plane's wingtip clipped off their roof.

The island tees are a memorable feature of the par-four 13th hole.

Stellenbosch

COURSE DESIGNER Ken Elkin
OPENED 1962

The finest moment for this historic Winelands golf club came when it was chosen to host the 1999 South African Open, and the championship was won by David Frost, who grew up in the town and learned to play golf on this parkland course. One of the men whose initiative helped secure the Open for Stellenbosch – the first time it had moved away from the traditional venues of either Royal Cape or Mowbray in the Western Cape – was then Sunshine Tour commissioner Arnold Mentz, now the club professional.

Stellenbosch had hosted Sunshine Tour events in the past – Frost also won the SA Masters there in 1987 – so it was a deserved selection. It again proved itself to be a demanding test with a winning score of 279, nine under on the revised par-72 layout.

While the golf club itself is more than a century old, the course is a lot younger, emerging on this site as a 1950s 9-holer by Bob Grimsdell, and then increased to 18 holes in 1962 with input from Ken Elkin. More recently it was upgraded by Mark Muller in time for the 2006 World Amateur Team Championships, which the club co-hosted with its neighbour De Zalze.

The club counts Stellenbosch University students among its members, and many of those Maties have been outstanding golfers who have represented South Africa at amateur level. When Frost won the SA Open at Stellenbosch, the reigning SA Amateur champion at the time was another club member, Jean Hugo, who received the Freddie Tait Cup as the leading amateur in 1999.

Stellenbosch lies on the crest of a hill, so it commands some impressive views, particularly from the par-three 7th, where the tee is roughly on the same level as the roof of the clubhouse, with the green far below. The previous hole encapsulates the beauty of golf in the Winelands, the approach shot to this par four having to be played across the corner of a vineyard to an elevated green. Doglegs like this one are a feature of a course where being able to shape shots can pay dividends. It is also a course where neither the intensity nor the attractiveness of the experience ever wanes, and a good front nine is followed by an even better back nine.

Mature trees line the fairways of the par-four 18th (left) and the par-four 1st (above) at this classic parkland course that hosted the 1999 South African Open.

Erinvale

COURSE DESIGNER Gary Player
OPENED 1995

Erinvale was the first golf estate launched in the Western Cape, in the mid-1990s, and its immediate success was the catalyst for many future developments in the region. Few estates anywhere in the world have a picturesque setting to match this. Built on the lower slopes of the towering Helderberg mountain that overlooks Somerset West, with stunning views over False Bay from higher aspects of the property, it has wine estates and fruit farms as neighbours on one side, and a nature reserve on the other.

Gary Player designed the course, a distinctive championship layout of two separate nines, the first meandering among the houses and water features in the flat land at the entrance to the estate, and the back nine climbing and falling among the hilly slopes. The higher you go, the more palatial the estate homes become. The routing has been cleverly conceived so that you seldom feel as if you are walking much uphill while playing, but by the time you get to the 15th tee you have reached a fairly high elevation. The estate itself goes even higher up the mountain.

In December 1996, eighteen months after it opened, the course was hosting the first-ever World Cup of Golf to be held in South Africa. The memorable tournament attracted some of the biggest crowds ever seen at a golf event in this country and was won in grand style for South Africa by Ernie Els and Wayne Westner. Erinvale has subsequently hosted two South African Opens, back to back in 2003 and 2004. Both were won by Trevor Immelman, who grew up in Somerset West and as a fifteen-year-old played Erinvale with Gary Player just before it opened.

Erinvale's design is unusual in that the finishing holes on each nine play side by side up to the attractive white clubhouse, framed against the backdrop of the Helderberg. Deep, steep-faced fairway bunkers separate the two fairways, and the greens of both holes stretch over 50 metres from front to back. Player copied famed American course architect Pete Dye in placing distinctive railway sleepers within bunkers on the course. The long par-four 17th is one of the most daunting holes in the game, playing downhill to a narrow green guarded by two pot bunkers. On the left are tall pine trees, while an out-of-bounds fence on the right is an even scarier proposition. It leaves you with a memorable impression of a challenging day's golf.

The tight par-four 17th plays down the slopes of the Helderberg mountain.

Steenberg

COURSE DESIGNER Peter Matkovich
OPENED 1996

Golf course living is very much a part of the South African residential scene, and the most exclusive estate of them all is Steenberg, primarily because of the remarkable value of the homes. The average selling price is higher here than anywhere else in South Africa, and the estate has proved a profitable investment for buyers since the Peter Matkovich golf course opened in 1996. Modest-looking homes sell today for over R20 million in some cases – something that has much to do with the fact that it is the only golf estate in Cape Town's affluent southern suburbs.

Steenberg is on the site of the Cape Peninsula's oldest farm, which produced its first wines in 1695, ten years after Groot Constantia, and is still productive today. Its north-facing vineyards on the slopes of the Constantiaberg mountain range are a feature on several of the golf holes that meander around the estate's single-storey homes. The course is predominantly parkland in design and feel, and nearly all the original waste bunkers have thankfully been removed and replaced by more strategic hazards, apart from one that is a questionable but distinctive feature of the par-five 12th. A rocky artificial stream was created to lend a different character to some of the holes.

Unusually for a golf estate, Steenberg resembles a private members' club – many of its members are not estate residents – and its comfortable single-storey clubhouse reflects a traditional ambience. Its 19th hole is a luxurious but jolly one, with an outside patio overlooking the green of the final hole, a par five guarded on the right by a water hazard. The clubhouse always has a festive atmosphere after golfing competitions. There is also a strong caddie culture, and many golfers prefer walking to driving in golf carts.

Matkovich set up the course to allow for the blustery Cape winds, making it playable in varying conditions. The subtle design variety is crucial in that respect, with the direction and length of hole constantly changing.

Many courses today claim a signature hole, yet Steenberg's signature is the consistency, attractiveness and balance of all 18 of its holes. The course is never too busy, and visitors are made welcome. There is an intimate five-star hotel at which to stay on the estate, part of the original seventeenth-century manor house.

The water feature of the par-three 7th hole (right) reflects the peaks of the Steenberg in the background. A mountain stream zigzags through the fairway of the par-five 18th (overleaf).

Clovelly

COURSE DESIGNER Charles Molteno Murray
OPENED 1934

Tucked away in a peaceful valley near Fish Hoek on the False Bay coast, this is one of the Cape Peninsula's most scenically attractive and aesthetically pleasing courses. It oozes charm and character from the moment you arrive at the attractive clubhouse and look down from the terrace on the course below. You tee off next to the clubhouse, with challenging drives into the valley. When golfing tourists started arriving from Europe in increased numbers in the 1990s, it was not surprising to see them flocking to Clovelly once this hideaway was discovered and the word about it began to spread.

Clovelly's advantage over other Cape courses is its relative remoteness, the quiet and solitude of playing there, and the natural surroundings – the Silvermine River that borders the property, sand dunes, indigenous bush, all overlooked by a rugged mountainside.

Less than 6 000 metres in length, with a par of 72, it is a friendly layout for the average handicap, without quite being a pushover thanks to the large trees that frame many of its holes. There is a lot to be said for courses like this one, where golf shots requiring accuracy and finesse, couched with an element of risk, are more rewarding than power. That is why they remain popular. The only drawback is that Clovelly is extremely busy during the summer.

Clovelly is proud to be known as one of the first clubs in South Africa to promote non-racial golf, having started out as one that welcomed both Jews and Christians, and has long maintained its own development programmes. The club has an interesting history dating back to the early 1930s, and its ownership has been linked to the Ackerman family of Pick n Pay fame since that time. Raymond Ackerman's father Gus purchased the land, and he had Charles Molteno Murray design the original 18 holes.

For years Clovelly was a rugged, sandy layout, until water reticulation transformed it over time into a lushly manicured course. Several holes have been modernised to increase the golfing challenge, so part of the old natural look has been lost to some extent, though this does not detract from the sheer delight of playing there. Only one par four is more than 400 metres, and the most demanding hole is the 9th, a par five starting on the lower slopes of the mountain and leading to an elevated green with some treacherous slopes.

The par-five 15th at Clovelly is one of the holes that have been modernised in recent years, with the green moved into the water hazard.

Milnerton

COURSE DESIGNER Golf Data
OPENED 1925

This scenic course occupies an enviably attractive position on the Atlantic Ocean, with several holes running above the sandy beach and stunning views towards Table Mountain. Because of the property's residential value it was converted in 1997 into a golf estate known as Sunset Links.

The old Milnerton was sandy and links-like, with holes sweeping between alien vegetation. It was a championship course, hugely affected by the wind, which hosted the SA Masters five times in the late 1970s and early 1980s, won by such luminaries as Gary Player, Mark McNulty (twice), Nick Price and Dale Hayes.

A new course, retaining some of the old routing – Milnerton is on a narrow stretch of land between the sea and a wetland waterway, and thus has nine holes out and nine back, similar to British links – was built by Golf Data to accommodate the estate. It still has a links feel on holes adjoining the dunes next to the beach, but the housing does at times intrude, particularly on the par-five 6th where a resident has taken the club to court over golf balls landing on his property. The course finishes with a strong par four running alongside the lagoon.

Pot bunkers on the par-three 7th (above) are a links feature at Milnerton. Not far away, waves crash on to the beach next to the par-four 2nd (below).

Atlantic Beach

COURSE DESIGNER Mark Muller
OPENED 2000

When the Royal & Ancient Golf Club decided to have qualifying tournaments for the Open Championship at international venues, the first one they visited in 2003 was Atlantic Beach. A rugged, windblown links-type course inside a golf estate, it closely matched the qualities required by Open Championship links golf.

On the West Coast next to the village of Melkbosstrand, Atlantic Beach has magnificent views of Table Bay, Table Mountain and Robben Island. The estate, like all those in the Cape, has been a success story, with 865 houses built since its launch at the close of the last century.

The Mark Muller-designed course, attractive and interesting as it is, has stirred some controversy, primarily because it has been routed through protected coastal fynbos. Many of the fairways, wide as they are, are lined by fynbos on either side, creating an intimidating tunnel effect for golfers in the windy conditions. The sensitive fynbos is a no-go area for golfers hoping to reclaim wayward balls. Yet Atlantic Beach rewards good shots and is a pleasure to play during the winter months, when most other courses in the Cape are waterlogged.

Robben Island is visible from the par-three 5th (above) and the full width of Table Mountain is in view on the par-three 12th (below).

Royal Cape

COURSE DESIGNER Charles Molteno Murray
OPENED 1906

As the oldest golf club in South Africa, founded in 1885, Royal Cape has always carried itself with suitable gravitas and responsibility. In 1910 it became the thirty-sixth golf club in the world to have the royal designation conferred upon it, and only the fifth outside Great Britain and Ireland. Several of its well-connected members served as presidents of the old South African Golf Union (SAGU), and six members have been crowned SA Amateur champion. Jack Watermeyer was both Amateur champion (1940) and president (1961–62).

The founder and first captain was Sir Henry Torrens, a British army officer who served in the Crimean War and Indian Mutiny, then became governor of the Cape Colony in 1886. An ardent golfer, he founded the Royal Malta Golf Club after leaving the Cape in 1888.

Royal Cape to this day is understated in a very British sort of way, having an unpretentious but smart single-storey clubhouse, a small but perfectly adequate changing room, lounges with large windows overlooking the 18th green and an elderly and refined membership. The 1st and 10th tees are but a few steps away from its hub; all is neat and orderly, polished and prim.

Golf has been played on this Wynberg/Ottery site for more than a century, making it the oldest course in continuous use, although routing changes have taken place over the years. In 1906 it was the first to have grass greens, on the recommendation of club member Charles Molteno Murray, South Africa's pioneer turf expert and an early course designer, who modified the layout into essentially its current shape in 1928.

Murray paved the way for other courses to replace gravel greens with grass, and in 1913 the SAGU ruled that their championships would only be held on courses with grass greens and tees. No fewer than ten South African Opens, the first in 1910 and the last in 1996, plus eight SA Amateur Championships, have been played at Royal Cape, giving the club a rich history.

The course is a flat, classic parkland layout sandwiched between busy roads and a railway line. It is restricted in terms of length but is still a considerable challenge with its tree-lined fairways, numerous doglegs, modern greens, good bunkering and water hazards. Straight driving is a prerequisite here. There are attractive views of the Cape Peninsula's mountain range, none more so than from the par-four 14th, a tiger in the southeaster.

The par-five 16th depicts the elegance of Royal Cape's classic parkland layout.

Arabella

COURSE DESIGNER Peter Matkovich
OPENED 1999

Arabella, near the seaside village of Hermanus, is the Western Cape's only golf resort, making it an attractive destination for visitors to Cape Town, which is just an hour's drive away. There are two travel options: the high road over Sir Lowry's Pass, or a longer detour along Clarence Drive, with its views across False Bay to the Cape Peninsula.

Inland from the ocean and susceptible to sea breezes, Arabella, with its five-star hotel, is both a resort and a golf estate. Attractive homes line the fairways on undulating land between the Kogelberg range and Bot River Lagoon, which is a focal point of the property.

Course designer Peter Matkovich has embraced the lagoon by having the finishing holes on each nine run alongside its wide and gentle waters. It makes for spectacular golf terrain. The course has been open for almost ten years and the German owners plan to complement it with an adjoining course.

Arabella has the look and feel of a resort, with generous playing corridors, white bunker sand framing the greens, and golfers in carts. Nevertheless, it is a challenging test for the good player, even more so when the wind blows during the summer. The course has troubled the professionals in Sunshine Tour events that have been played there in recent years. From the championship tees it is 6 381 metres. The tougher holes come early on, at the inland 3rd, 4th and 6th, all exacting par fours in terms of length and difficulty.

The intimate clubhouse is on the ground floor of the five-storey Western Cape Hotel & Spa, and the 1st hole climbs away from the lagoon to reach the parkland features of the estate. The course descends again with a wonderful par five, the 8th, tumbling in stages to a green in the heart of a wetland area. These holes by the lagoon are both scenic and adventurous to play. Two of them, 9 and 16, are shortish par fours where you can risk all with your driver or play cautiously. The round ends with a par three, the 17th, edging the lagoon, and a long curving par five following the shoreline, where a sinuous bunker is the only barrier preventing your golf ball from disappearing into the wetland.

In 2007 the International Association of Golf Tour Operators named Arabella the Golf Resort of the Year in the Rest of the World category (outside Europe and North America). The course's strength is the sheer variety of the golfing experience, each hole presenting a new surprise.

The breathtaking par-five 8th hole is one of the country's most stunning.

The Bot River Lagoon forms the backdrop to some fabulous holes at Arabella. Clockwise from top left: both the 16th and 9th are tempting, short par fours, while the par-five 18th runs parallel to the edge of the lagoon.

Hermanus

COURSE DESIGNER Peter Matkovich
OPENED 2006

It is not uncommon to find an old golf clubhouse being bulldozed and a larger, more functional structure erected on the site, but you will find very few instances anywhere in the world of a golf club choosing to dig up the golf course that had served it well for many years, and replacing it with an entirely different, modern layout.

One South African club bold enough to do just that was Hermanus. Their 2003 decision to take charge of their future has given them an outstanding 18-hole championship track, and an extra 9-hole facility, both designed by Peter Matkovich. It was all completed in good time for the club's 2007 centenary.

The original course at Hermanus was an enjoyable Bob Grimsdell layout that seemed a natural fit for a sleepy seaside resort that had not yet really noticed the whales cavorting off the coastline. Holidaymakers and the mostly retired members loved it for the way it flattered their scores, but over the years the permanent populace steadily grew, swelling Hermanus and its surrounding villages into a fair-sized town. Sandwiched as it was between mountains and the ocean, the town's residential land was becoming increasingly valuable. The opportunity was there to develop and expand the old golf course into a modern golf estate, and it was promptly seized.

Golf at Hermanus is seasonal, and having 27 holes now allows the club to cater for more golfers during the holiday periods. The main course ventures into an area that is outside the confines of the original layout, rising and falling to give stunning views over Walker Bay. It is a tremendous improvement on the old one – bolder, more exciting and exhilarating to play. Yet, with its extra length and contoured, modern greens, it can also be difficult in windy conditions. Matkovich has allowed for that with a variety of tees on each hole, which make it playable for a disparate range of golfers.

The course's new stature has seen the club host several championships. The Interprovincial returned there in 2008 for the first time in 36 years.

Hermanus still retains the pine forests and natural sandy vegetation that were its original features, and the trees on the new layout are much more of a factor than they were before. For instance, a forest of these trees provides a remarkable tunnel effect on the par-five 11th, which is just one of several splendid signature holes.

The seaside town of Hermanus and the golf club are nestled below the Kleinrivier mountains.

THE
garden route

Spectacular, breathtaking and inspiring are just a few of the adjectives used to describe the scenic new golf courses on this rugged stretch of coastline between Mossel Bay in the west and Plettenberg Bay in the east, where mountain ranges create an impressive backdrop. Although the Garden Route was once regarded by some as a rural backwater, a golf course construction boom has transformed it into a golfing mecca for visitors, a reputation boosted by a pleasant climate that makes golf possible twelve months of the year.

It all started with the development of the world-class Fancourt resort in the early 1990s, offering golf of an enviably high quality at three differenct courses. The trend has continued with the building of golf estates and resorts on a variety of dramatic sites overlooking the Indian Ocean. Playing along towering clifftops at Pinnacle Point near Mossel Bay, named one of the world's best new courses, is a memorable golfing experience, as is driving the ball high in the hills at Simola above the Knysna Lagoon or on the headlands of Pezula.

George, a relatively small town with six 18-hole courses of its own, is the main hub of the region, with an airport connected to all the major centres. Courses along the Garden Route have been designed by a who's who of the architectural world – Gary Player, Peter Matkovich, Ernie Els, David McLay Kidd and Jack Nicklaus.

Pinnacle Point

COURSE DESIGNER Peter Matkovich
OPENED 2006

No South African course has created quite such a buzz within the international golfing community as Pinnacle Point near Mossel Bay. It was named one of the ten best new courses in the world soon after opening, and acclaim for its rugged beauty and dramatic holes has made it one of the most talked-about golfing destinations.

The reason for the hullabaloo is simple: no golf course designer before Peter Matkovich had previously been given the opportunity to work on such an extremely high site next to the ocean, and to build a continuous stretch of holes that hop and skip for a few kilometres, from the edge of one sheer cliff to another, suspended above pounding surf. It took Matkovich's bold and creative thinking even to contemplate the possibility of laying out 18 holes on steeply sloping rocky terrain that seemed ill suited for the game of golf.

Matkovich has succeeded spectacularly by letting his imagination run wild, and allowing the terrain to dictate the flow of the course. He found room for three adventurous par threes on the cliffs, greens perched perilously close to the edge, created a short par four where the direct route to the green requires a 200-metre carry over a rocky inlet, and finished with a risk-and-reward par five banking along the side of the cliffs to its green on a headland.

The clubhouse at Pinnacle Point complements the inspired setting. A circular triple-storey structure built on the headland overlooking the 9th and 18th greens, it has views to the east and the west along the coastline. In the bay below, whales and dolphins can be spotted at different times of the year.

Limited space on the headland means golfers either have to drive a cart to the clubhouse (carts are compulsory), or arrange a lift from the reception area/practice range at the top of the hill down to the course. Pinnacle Point is exclusive in the sense that only members and guests, homeowners and people staying on the estate have access to the course; there is no pay-and-play option for day visitors.

The opening holes climb inland away from the clubhouse before turning and falling back towards the ocean. There are thrilling drops in elevation before you reach the cliffs and play the short par-three 7th, a flick wedge to a green on a rocky promontory. The back nine is routed in a figure of eight along the coastline, each hole having its own spectacular view.

Pinnacle Point boasts some of South Africa's most dramatic golf holes, like the par-three 7th.

Both nines at Pinnacle Point include holes that are high up on the estate, then circle back down and play along the cliff edge. Clockwise from top left: the par-four 4th plays along a ridge with views west along the coast; the par-three 13th requires plenty of nerve and focus; the par-three 17th features organic shaping and bunkering.

Oubaai

COURSE DESIGNER Ernie Els
OPENED 2005

It was fitting that Ernie Els's first course design in South Africa should be sited on this open headland above the seaside village of Herold's Bay, where his family have owned holiday homes for many years. Els's private jet can often be seen parked at George Airport nearby. His love for the Garden Route began in 1991 when he shared a house in Mossel Bay with friends during a Sunshine Tour event at Fancourt. His father Neels afterwards bought John Bland's home in Herold's Bay, and Ernie acquired a stand in front of it. That became the site of the first house he built.

Oubaai is an estate/resort course developed by a Kuwaiti company, and the routing was designed to accommodate two separate clubhouses, one overlooking the 18th hole and the ocean for estate homeowners and club members, and the other inland, next to the Lifestyle Centre, golf academy and 10th tee, where visitors begin their rounds. A hundred-room Hyatt Regency hotel is also now part of this vibrant area, and is home to the first-ever South African Golf Hall of Fame.

Oubaai was meant to be the first of three golf estate developments on the coastline near George, but it was the only one to secure planning approval, while adjacent courses by Greg Norman and Retief Goosen have been delayed.

The course reflects Els's modern design thinking, incorporating length and strategic play, with the attractive and prominent bunkering a dominant feature of the layout. The exposed nature of the terrain – there are very few trees – and the mounding and rough grasses between holes lend an almost links-type quality in places, particularly in the breezy conditions that prevail along this coastline, although the many homes on the property tend to spoil that effect.

The Gwaing River valley runs next to Oubaai, and the course has sensational views into the deep gorge, none more so than on the testing 6th hole, a long par three played over indigenous bush on the edge of the precipice. The holes next to the river valley are some of the course's most scenic. Another memorable par three comes on the 17th, with the ocean as a backdrop. The round ends with an unusual dogleg par five high above the cove called Oubaai.

Wind is always a factor at the coast, especially on the par-three 17th hole (above). The par-four 5th (right) plays towards the Gwaing River valley.

The Links at Fancourt

COURSE DESIGNER Gary Player
OPENED 2000

For sheer genius of golf course architecture and creative thinking, few courses in the world can match this artificial links layout. Gary Player, with the help of assistant designer Phil Jacobs, took a flat piece of land adjoining the Fancourt resort near George and recreated all the attributes of a dramatic links that would not be out of place in Scotland or Ireland. In fact, if built in either of those countries, the course would have received more worldwide acclaim than it has. Player, who loves links golf but has never had the opportunity to design a natural links, considers it his golf design masterpiece.

Fancourt owner Hasso Plattner wanted a golf course that would be judged among the best in the world, so no expense was spared in building The Links. Plattner himself spent time providing input, and was just as passionate as the design and construction team about what was taking shape. Mountains of sand were trucked in to create the high dunes between holes, which are a feature of any great links. Rough native grasses were planted, and the links concept quickly took shape. Within a few years of being opened, the course was hosting the biggest tournament ever to come to South Africa, the 2003 Presidents Cup match.

Bringing together twenty-four of the world's best players, this biennial contest between an International team and a team from the United States was a major coup for both Fancourt and Plattner. It also meant that Player got to captain the International team for the first time at a course he had designed himself. The match was memorable, with the teams tied 16–16 after four days' play. Then Tiger Woods and Ernie Els went out just before sunset in a sudden-death play-off to try to decide the outcome. After two tense holes it was too dark to continue, and the spoils were justly shared.

The Links is the most challenging test of golf in South Africa because of the sheer range of hazards throughout its 18 holes. It has Scottish burns, pot bunkers, natural wetlands, undulating fairways and subtly contoured greens. There is no let up at any stage, and at 6 930 metres (par 73) from the back tees it is punishingly long for a sea-level course. The Presidents Cup was matchplay,

The par-four 10th hole is one of the many challenging holes on this championship layout.

47

so no medal scores were posted, but two years later, in December 2005, the South African Open came to The Links and only four players bettered par for 72 holes.

Two of South Africa's finest golfers, Retief Goosen and Els, had a final-round duel to remember in the annals of the championship. Playing together, with the rest of the field lying far behind them, Goosen was three ahead of Els with five to play. Then Els was able to birdie three consecutive holes from the 14th to the 16th and tie proceedings as they walked to the 17th, a treacherous par three known as Prayer. (Each hole at The Links has a name, in true old-fashioned links tradition.)

The pin was on the back right shelf of a long green guarded on the left by a deep burn with a sheer stone wall. One player had actually fallen in there during the Open, having ventured too close to the edge. Both Els and Goosen missed the green with their tee shots.

Goosen short-sided himself over the back, and was looking at a miraculous recovery just to save par. He conjured an amazing chip shot that went into the hole for a birdie two. Els was stunned, but kept his poise, and his own chip only just stayed out. The drama was not yet over. After two magnificent shots up the par-five 18th close to the pin, Els had a reasonably short eagle putt to tie and force a play-off – only to miss his opportunity. There was thus no play-off, as there had been at the Presidents Cup.

The Links is a private club, separate from the resort, although a limited number of tee times are available for Fancourt guests. The large L-shaped clubhouse has its own exclusive members' section. The links feel is immediately evident around the starter's hut and 1st tee, and golfers have a sense of being transported into another world. It will be 18 holes before a fourball and their caddies – no golf carts are allowed – return to the clubhouse, because the halfway house is in the middle of the course.

The opening two holes are suitably surreal and challenging for anyone who has not played links golf before. The second, aptly named Lang Drop, is one of the great par threes in golf, 196 metres from its elevated club tee to a green of devilish slopes. White sand lies scattered among high dunes on the left, and there is a fine view of the main Fancourt dam. There are 15 holes on the other side of the causeway, and each one provides a distinctive experience.

Authentic links golf is combined with beautiful water features on the par-four 15th hole (left). The par-four 12th hole (overleaf) is called Sheer Murrrder and is the stroke one on the course.

Fancourt Montagu

COURSE DESIGNERS Gary Player/David McLay Kidd
OPENED 1992

Fancourt is one of the world's leading golf resorts/estates, and the Montagu has always been regarded as its premier resort course. To enhance its appeal and strengthen it as a modern layout, it was given a major makeover by promising young Scottish course architect David McLay Kidd during 2004. The course was closed for more than a year as McLay Kidd, whose name is attached to a string of famous layouts in the United States and Britain, transformed the original Gary Player design into something more of his own making.

The Montagu layout was opened in 1992 and was a revelation at that time for South African golfers, for whom new courses – certainly of this calibre – were few and far between. It introduced them to modern bunkering and greens comparable in terms of slickness, slopes and speed to Augusta National itself, and it heralded an exciting new era in innovative golf course design.

With its American ideas, including a golf director straight from Texas in the person of Jeff Clause, Fancourt also brought with it another concept with which South Africans were unfamiliar – exclusivity. The only golfers allowed to play at the Montagu are members, hotel residents and guests of estate homeowners. No one can walk in off the street and pay a green fee.

Fancourt was the benchmark for conditioning among South African golf courses, and we owe the quality of greens in this country today to what the Fancourt maintenance team was achieving during most of the 1990s. It inspired other clubs to emulate the Montagu, with results that are now apparent all over the country.

McLay Kidd's first brief was to eliminate a weak opening hole on the Montagu, a short par four that threaded its way between houses and was a nightmare opening tee shot for nervous golfers. Homes on either side were peppered with golf balls. He built a new 1st hole on what used to be the par-five 9th, and created another par five to finish off the front nine. Apart from that, the course resembles its predecessor, except that the greens have been modernised and new sets of hazards have been introduced. Some of the quirkier design features have been removed.

The Montagu is a glorious parkland layout, covering large tracts of varying terrain on rolling land. Its beauty is enhanced by mature trees, flower beds, shrubs and water hazards that provide a colourful contrast to the landscape.

The par-five 9th hole is one of the new holes built when the Montagu was redesigned in 2004.

The exquisitely conditioned Montagu course is at the heart of the award-winning Fancourt resort. Clockwise from top left: the par-three 2nd hole is played from a high tee; prominent bunkering and an avenue of trees protect the par-four 14th; and a small stream crosses the fairway and runs into the pond of the bold par-five 10th.

Fancourt Outeniqua

COURSE DESIGNER Gary Player
OPENED 1997

Fancourt started out with the one 18-hole course in 1991, and another 9 holes were added a year later. It remained a 27-hole facility for five years before enough land was acquired from a neighbouring farmer to complete 36 holes in 1997 and have two separate courses, the Montagu and Outeniqua.

The latter is named after the mountain range that overlooks the area, while its neighbour gets its title from the famed Montagu Pass that was the first road to cross the range from George through to the Karoo beyond. Today it is a provincial heritage site and remains an alternative and scenic way of travelling between George and Oudtshoorn. The pass was completed in 1847 under the supervision and leadership of two men, Henry Fancourt White and John Montagu. White, who named his son Montagu, later built a family home at Blanco, and this old manor house is today part of the resort.

In its early years Fancourt hosted three Sunshine Tour events. The last of these was held in 1995 and won by Ernie Els, who has retained a connection with the resort as a playing ambassador and has based his foundation there. The tournament 18 for those events comprised what is today mainly the back nine of the Outeniqua layout and the final nine holes of the Montagu. These were the first 18 holes opened for play, and were regarded as the championship set-up.

Because of the way in which it came together in two halves over a long time, the Outeniqua has a different look from the Montagu, so they complement each other perfectly as varying playing experiences. The Outeniqua is regarded as the easier course of the two, being more open in appearance on the new section, yet it has its share of challenges and risk-and-reward moments. Water hazards or streams come into play on as many as eleven of the holes, including the last five.

Fancourt was open farmland to start with, and the character of the courses has benefited from the planting of hundreds of mature trees on the estate, mostly bought by Fancourt owner Hasso Plattner after he took ownership in 1994. He is said to have acquired no less than 400 oaks, many saved from the chainsaw, and had them delivered from various parts of the Cape.

The par-five 7th (above) follows the wooded river boundary of the estate. The Outeniqua mountains form a backdrop to the par-five 17th (right) and the par-three 4th (overleaf).

George

COURSE DESIGNER Charles Molteno Murray
OPENED 1931

The Garden Route is full of spectacular new golf courses, but one layout that remains universally popular with golfers visiting the region is the granddaddy of them all, George Golf Club in the heart of this provincial centre. Overlooked by the Outeniqua mountains, it is a parkland gem that has given many golfers the most pleasant rounds of their lives.

Yet George is also the most dynamic of golf clubs, and the course has certainly not stood still in recent years. Although all the features that everyone enjoys most about it have been retained, there have been substantial changes and improvements to keep it modern and relevant, in keeping with the phenomenal growth of the region.

The town of George was a sleepy backwater until the opening of Fancourt precipitated a boom in the 1990s. Resort visitors liked what they saw around them, and it was no coincidence that George Golf Club started to move with the times. The club had a classic tree-lined 1930s design by Charles Molteno Murray that contrasted sharply with the design of Fancourt, but was highly appreciated by European visitors, who referred to it as the 'Old Course'.

George had become a thickly wooded layout, with dense vegetation and trees bordering its holes to the extent that the outside world was hidden from view, but a combination of events helped open it up and provide more scenic vistas. There had been property developments on neighbouring land, including the new Kingswood golf estate, and in 1999 the club made a momentous decision that would transform the aesthetics of the property. A bushy wasteland of alien vegetation in front of the clubhouse, which hid much of the course, was cleared and replaced by a vast new dam bordering the 1st, 17th and 18th holes. It was incredible what a difference this made to the outlook from the clubhouse, while also notably improving the opening hole, previously an undistinguished short par four. Water left of the fairway not only makes for a sensational looking hole, but also a challenging opening tee shot.

Thanks to its improvements, George was awarded the 2002 SA Amateur Championship. It has an unusually varied routing. The front nine has seven par fours, while the back nine includes three par threes and three par fives. Strikingly individual holes and sloping fairways add to the overall character.

The par-four opening hole skirts a large dam at George Golf Club. The dam also borders the 17th and 18th holes.

Simola

COURSE DESIGNER Jack Nicklaus
OPENED 2005

The story of this new resort/estate course high in the hills above Knysna has been a long-running saga, outlining the problems that can ruin any golf estate developer. While the dreams of one man were shattered, others have triumphed in getting Simola to where it is today, one of the most breathtakingly beautiful resorts in Africa.

Jack Nicklaus was involved from the beginning in 1995 when original developer Ola Grinaker presented his vision of what he wanted to accomplish on his farmland – a golfing paradise in an area of natural beauty with unsurpassed views of the Knysna Lagoon and surrounding countryside. But ten years were to pass between Nicklaus first visiting the site, to a fanfare of media attention, and the final opening of the course that had brought heartbreak to many.

Grinaker's venture took shape in the 1980s when he had local experts assess the site. Even then he wanted Nicklaus as the designer, but the timing was not right politically or economically. The dream became reality in the early days of the golf estate boom when Nicklaus signed for a $1 million design fee, plus expenses, a remarkable amount then.

Two years later the development was bankrupt, following a deluge of rain in 1996 that washed topsoil off the estate into the Knysna Lagoon, creating an environmental disaster. Simola was liquidated, with debts of R51 million. After standing idle for five years it was bought on auction for a fraction of that amount by Avril Kaschula of Kat Leisure. Crucially, with the help of Golf Data – original partners with Grinaker – he got Nicklaus back to complete the course.

Being in the hills, Simola has limited room for 18 holes, so it essentially lies in two separate valleys and you need a golf cart to get around its majestic parkland holes, with an unusual configuration of five par threes and five par fives. After playing the opening hole you climb a steep hill to the 2nd tee, which looks down from a thrilling height into the next valley to the green of a short par four, positioned close to where Grinaker had his farmhouse. There are six holes here, with eye-catching views over the Knysna River.

Simola delights the golfer with its stunning scenery and superb conditioning, plus the simple beauty and generous playability of the Nicklaus design. By the end of 2007 a luxury hotel stood on high ground overlooking the main valley.

Dramatic changes in elevation combine with magnificent scenery on the par-four 2nd (left) and the par-three 6th (overleaf).

Pezula

COURSE DESIGNERS David Dale/Ronald Fream
OPENED 2000

Pezula was the first of the 'jaw-dropping' golf resorts/estates along the Garden Route, where stupendous scenic beauty wrapped up in a challengingly diverse golf course captured the hearts and imagination of golfers and homeowners. The estate has grown to embrace 1 000 hectares of prime location on a rugged stretch of coastline east of the Knysna Heads. One of its most desirable properties is the Pezula Private Castle on Noetzie Beach, where guests are spoiled by a resident chef, housekeeper and butler. Pezula's special qualities as a place to stay have seen it garnering numerous international accolades. In 2008 it was voted Best Property in the World at the CNBC International Property Awards, judged on location, architectural design, appearance and finish. Pezula was also named Africa's Leading Spa Resort in 2008, just three years after the spa was opened along with the resort's luxury five-star hotel.

The Golfplan team of Americans David Dale and Ronald Fream, an experienced veteran who once worked under Robert Trent Jones, created an expansive layout that works with different aspects of the topography to provide 360-degree views. This is not just spectacular oceanfront golf but a striking blend of scenic experiences. Situated high on a headland, it provides views of indigenous forest, floral fynbos, the Knysna Lagoon and the ocean.

It is a long and undulating course, so golf carts are compulsory most of the time, although walking is allowed for twilight rounds in summer. There are steep climbs where carts come into their own in getting you to the next tee. The extreme nature of the terrain, particularly on the coastal section, and the fact that the developers had to work within strict environmental parameters, means every hole has elevation changes, adding to their individuality. Aesthetics are supreme here, yet the course also has stunning design variety.

A feature is the five different tees on each hole, making it playable for everyone, and there is only one water hazard, on the 2nd. There are enough other hazards to catch you out, although their severity is balanced off the tee. The views on the back nine, as you head for the ocean, are remarkable, as are the holes. The 12th and 13th plunge almost 100 metres in height, until you reach a green on the edge of the cliffs, while the short par-four 14th is possibly the most photographed hole in South Africa.

The par-four 12th (left) and the par-three 3rd (overleaf) at Pezula, east of the famous Knysna Heads, command stunning views over the Indian Ocean.

Goose Valley

COURSE DESIGNER Gary Player
OPENED 1996

Gary Player's Plettenberg Bay holiday home has beautiful views over the Keurbooms Lagoon and Tsitsikamma coastline. Since the mid-1990s it has also been part of the Goose Valley golf estate, which started out as a 9-holer, and stayed that way for seven years before being extended to 18 holes, the full layout opening in 2003.

It is a charmingly attractive course, enjoyed by residents and holidaymakers for the welcoming friendliness of both the layout (just under 6 000 metres from the back tees) and the club staff. The cosy clubhouse has an attractive terrace overlooking the 18th, one of two short par fours to finish the round.

The original 9 holes are mixed with the new ones, and are among the most appealing because they run through protected natural areas of the estate. The par-three 11th is one of the Garden Route's treasures, having a well-bunkered and wide green amid the indigenous bush, set against a backdrop of the lagoon and the ocean beyond.

Most of the new holes are within the Turtle Creek housing development, and while they are challenging they do not possess quite the same character as the original holes. Two longish par fours start each nine, but the hole that commands the most respect is the par-five 7th, doglegging left around a water hazard.

Goose Valley has a blend of links and parkland features, and rolling fairways and pot bunkers characterise the par-five 7th hole (above) and the par-three 11th hole (right).

THE
sunshine
& wild coasts

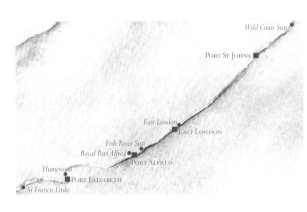

Wild Coast Sun
PORT ST JOHNS
East London
EAST LONDON
Fish River Sun
Royal Port Alfred
PORT ALFRED
Humewood
PORT ELIZABETH
St Francis Links

With its myriad attractions, the remote Eastern Cape has come into its own as a holiday destination. Here you can enjoy golf at some of South Africa's most classic coastal layouts, laze on a string of superb beaches, take in the best surfing waves in the world, and visit malaria-free game reserves.

There is a substantial golfing tradition here, as this was where the game flourished in the last decade of the nineteenth century, well ahead of other parts of the country. Port Elizabeth Golf Club was founded in 1890 and East London Golf Club in 1893. The courses in this region often have a quirky, old-fashioned feel to them, as at Royal Port Alfred. The province is home to the only two natural links in South Africa, at historic Humewood on the shores of Algoa Bay and the more modern St Francis Links further west, designed by Jack Nicklaus in the vast sand dunes close to Cape St Francis. The surfing paradise of Jeffreys Bay is a short drive away.

Game reserves abound in the dry scrubby inland bush, from Kwandwe with its prolific wildlife, including the Big Five, to the exclusive Shamwari where Tiger Woods and his wife Elin announced their engagement after the 2003 Presidents Cup, and Addo Elephant National Park closer to Port Elizabeth. New inland estate courses near these reserves include Katberg and the Gary Player-designed course at Bushman Sands.

St Francis Links

COURSE DESIGNER Jack Nicklaus
OPENED 2006

South Africa doubled its tally of natural links courses when Jack Nicklaus created this formidable championship layout in the vast dunefields overlooking St Francis Bay, having discovered the site more than ten years before. Until then, Humewood had been the only local links that could claim to be one of the 170 or so authentic versions in the world. Their rarity value can be measured against 34 000 courses worldwide.

The origins of the game stem from links golf. Centuries ago it was the only form of golf, played on rough, natural terrain close to the sea, against the elements. The imperfections of the land meant that bounces were unpredictable, and today that remains the essential difference between a links and a parkland layout.

Many of the new courses built over the last twenty years are of a familiar and similar design, but St Francis Links is unique. When Nicklaus was first brought here on a mid-1990s visit to the Eastern Cape, he knew that he could not pass up the opportunity to build 18 holes on such a naturally flowing canvas; few designers are given such pristine linksland on which to be creative.

The beauty of St Francis Links lies in the way the course magically unfolds over the dunes. The terrain is rugged and diverse, intricately varied in its challenges, and the rustic Nicklaus bunkering complements the natural features. Nicklaus even introduced two separate greens on the par-four 4th hole, where he was so conflicted over what to do that he could not leave without creating an alternative green higher up in the dunes.

The Eastern Cape coastline is notoriously windy, and St Francis Links is best explored for the first time in calm conditions. It takes time to understand the course and to gain confidence.

There is a surprising amount of water on the estate, certainly not what you would expect on a links. Three holes on the back nine encircle a vast lake, and other water hazards come into play on the par-three 7th and par-four 18th. The reason for all the water is that when the developers removed hundreds of hectares of alien vegetation from the dunes, the water table rose, and the underground Sand River now flows more regularly. Nicklaus was thrilled with the finished product. 'It's not the best course I've designed, it's the best course I've seen.' Quite a compliment coming from him.

The par-four 5th hole plays from high up on a dune down to a well-protected green.

This modern links course is built in the dunes of St Francis Bay. Clockwise from top left: the par-three 7th hole has a narrow green that places a premium on distance control; rugged, natural bunkers surround the par-four 18th green below the clubhouse; the seaside town of St Francis Bay is visible over the par-four 1st green.

Humewood

COURSE DESIGNER Colonel SV Hotchkin
OPENED 1931

The world was about to enter the Great Depression when Colonel Stafford Vere Hotchkin, a Lincolnshire landowner and British army officer in the First World War, embarked on a voyage to South Africa in 1929 that would leave us with a lasting golf legacy.

Hotchkin, already in his fifties, was a relatively inexperienced golf architect looking for work. In all probability this was why he agreed to design a second course for the Port Elizabeth Golf Club (PEGC) in a snake-infested wilderness of sand dunes and bush near Cape Recife. Fortunately for the PEGC, Hotchkin was heavily influenced by the work of Harry Colt, regarded as the father of British golf course design. He applied the Colt design philosophy of natural symmetry with the land to his new project, so creating an enduring masterpiece at Humewood. News spread of what Hotchkin had achieved on the shores of Algoa Bay, and he went on to make substantial improvements at Maccauvlei and East London, other classic designs from that era.

Within three years of Humewood's 1931 opening it was hosting the South African Open, and it has been a regular tournament venue ever since. It has had five SA Opens, the most recent of those in 2006, which was won by Ernie Els, and ten SA Amateur Championships, plus numerous Sunshine Tour events.

Humewood remained part of the PEGC for almost twenty years before becoming a separate club in 1952. It has one of the most striking clubhouses in South Africa, a beautiful white double-storey building situated in the middle of the links, with incomparable views over the course from its top-floor bar.

Unlike in Britain, where links often follow a ribbon-like routing along the shoreline, Hotchkin had ample space on which to build. He divided his course into two separate nines, one on either side of the clubhouse. The strong winds influenced his choice of routing. Most of the holes run east to west so that golfers are either playing into or with the wind, rather than having to deal with unpleasant cross-winds, but it is a course where you constantly change direction. His unusual design contained no fewer than eight par fives, and they stayed that way until the 1970s, when four became long par fours. There are wide fairways and few bunkers, so Humewood generally needs a wind to defend itself. When a rare calm descended on the 2006 SA Open, Ernie Els broke the championship scoring record with a 24-under-par 264.

Humewood's par-five 11th is typical of this classic old links course, host to many tournaments.

East London

COURSE DESIGNERS George Peck/Colonel SV Hotchkin
OPENED 1923

The East London course is where Ernie Els first came to prominence as a skinny sixteen-year-old at the 1986 SA Amateur Championship. Els, the youngest winner since Bobby Locke in 1935, enchanted local crowds with fearless, spectacular golf as he went on to win the title. It marked him out as a future major champion.

East London's superbly varied layout is built on one of the finest natural sites anywhere in the world, and it remains unspoiled and undeveloped, remote from the busy outside world. It climbs and undulates over high forested dunes and through thick indigenous bush on the Indian Ocean shoreline, overlooking some of the finest beaches in the country between the Buffalo and Nahoon rivers. From its highest tees and greens the course offers splendid vistas over the sea and along the coastline.

East London, together with Durban Country Club and Humewood, forms part of a triumvirate of uniquely classic championship courses that have left an indelible impression on the history of golf in South Africa. The three have hosted an amazing twenty-nine SA Opens and thirty-one SA Amateurs, sixty national championships in all. These three courses were the foundation on which our golfing traditions were built from the 1920s onward, and the clubs' members have contributed much to the fabric of the game in this country.

While each course was originally laid out by a different man, Colonel Stafford Vere Hotchkin (of Humewood fame) was influential in redesign work at both East London and Durban CC not many years after they were opened for play. Hotchkin's vision gave East London its distinctive great holes, of which the 9th is one. The reason why the course today has only three par threes is that he eliminated one in 1930 to create what is today's 4th hole.

There are several similarities between the East London and Durban CC courses — the holes in valleys between tropical bush, elevated greens and tees, the quirkiness and character of some of the holes, tightly guarded greens, and having halfway houses some distance from the clubhouse to cater for old-fashioned routing. The two courses are also comparable in total length from the championship tees — at about 6 150 metres — and both have several shortish par fours by modern standards. Today they also share paspalum grass on their greens.

The par-four 6th hole is reachable from the tee if the winds are favourable.

Their list of champions is equally impressive. Winners at East London, apart from Els, have included Sid Brews, Bobby Locke, Reg Taylor, Gary Player, Mark McNulty and Retief Goosen.

East London, situated in one of the smaller and less affluent centres, does not experience the constant flow of golfing traffic we see elsewhere, but remains a progressive club. It was left off the South African Open roster for three decades, when the old South African Golf Union selfishly restricted themselves to the three main centres of Johannesburg, Durban and Cape Town. The club's committee broke the trend when they brought the Open back in 2000, with the help of sponsors Mercedes Benz, one of the city's major manufacturers.

The clubhouse and surrounding infrastructure was modernised at that time, and in 2008 the venerable layout was updated with new greens and additional bunkering under the supervision of Cape Town course architect Mark Muller. To replace the local cynodon, which had been there for more than eighty years, a new strain of paspalum grass was planted on the greens for the first time. Although Muller did move the position of one green, the 13th, he stayed true to the design heritage of George Peck, the original architect in 1923, and Hotchkin. Today the club is host to the Africa Open, one of the four biggest tournaments on the Sunshine Tour.

Historic progressiveness at East London can also be found in the fact that it was the venue where Indian golfing legend Papwa Sewgolum was allowed to play in his first South African Open in 1961. In apartheid-era South Africa, he needed a permit to travel from Natal to the Eastern Cape, and was not allowed to enter the clubhouse (he changed in his car), but he did compete and finished sixteenth.

Just eleven years later, also at East London, black golfers played in the SA Amateur Championship for the first time. Ronald Ngqaka, a caddie at the club, was one of the thirty-two matchplay qualifiers, and had the distinction of beating a Springbok, Johann Murray. A club member, Robin Gouverneur, who won the club championship nine times, reached the final that year, losing to Neville Sundelson. In 1977, another caddie, Alfred Makandla, played in and won the Border matchplay title at his home course, beating sporting legend Buster Farrer in the final.

It was altogether fitting then that in 1993, when the SA Amateur was back at East London, the winner should be none other than eighteen-year-old Zimbabwean Lewis Chitengwa, the first black man to win the national crown. Tragically, Chitengwa died only eight years later from a rare form of meningitis while playing golf on the Canadian Tour.

East London has some great par-fives built over undulating dunes and through thick coastal vegetation. Good examples are the 1st (left) and 11th holes (overleaf).

83

Fish River Sun

COURSE DESIGNER Gary Player
OPENED 1990

Anyone visiting this remote and often deserted coastal course midway between Port Elizabeth and East London will wonder how it ever came to be developed in such an isolated area. There is an easy answer: one-armed bandits, blackjack and roulette. Fish River Sun was created by Sun International at a time when the government did not permit casinos to be built in cities but allowed them to be erected in outlying areas, where they were evidently less of a temptation to gamblers.

Casinos and golf went together like strawberries and cream then, and Fish River Sun's modern Player design proved popular with Eastern Cape golfers. Today, its casino licence has been lost to Port Elizabeth, and all that remains is the hotel, but the challenging layout still hosts the occasional tournament, notably the 2008 Africa Open on the Sunshine Tour.

Fish River Sun has memorable holes, especially those that bring the Old Woman's River into play. You have to hit shots across it twice on the back nine, and it is a feature of the par-five 12th, which curves sharply around the river's banks. The course's isolation is part of its charm. It winds through coastal bush, and while the sea is often hidden by high dunes, you feel its breezes.

The par-three 8th (above) is a short hole played over a small dam. The par-five 16th (below) requires a lengthy carry over the Old Woman's River to reach the green.

Royal Port Alfred

COURSE DESIGNER Unknown
OPENED 1907

For a feel of how seaside golf used to be played in an altogether different era of hickory shafts, persimmon heads and the small ball, Royal Port Alfred is the closest you will come in South Africa to experiencing a timeless sense of playing the game. The South African Open was held here in 1922. While the course is now more lushly grassed than in earlier years, it still resembles the layout played by our golfing ancestors. And members refer to the holes by their names — Whale's Back, Hippo's Bath, Punch Bowl — rather than numbers.

You have to contend with blind holes, sloping fairways and firm greens, and the rugged terrain is more suited to matchplay. The club, a hundred years old in 2007, retains old traditions, and its biggest tournament is the Kelly Foursomes, an annual inter-club gathering of players from the Eastern Province Golf Union contesting a form of the game that is waning in popularity. It is named after one of South African golf's great benefactors, the late Hugh Kelly, a Port Alfred institution.

Port Alfred was the last of the four Royal clubs in South Africa to celebrate its centenary (for which modern clubhouse extensions were built), yet it received Royal status in 1924, well before Johannesburg (1931) and Durban (1932).

Sloping fairways and coastal winds on the par-three 11th (above) and the par-five 18th (below) are part of the challenge at Royal Port Alfred.

Wild Coast Sun

COURSE DESIGNER Robert Trent Jones Junior
OPENED 1983

The tee shot on the 18th hole at the Wild Coast Sun is a memorable one, played from a high slope across a wide expanse of water to the fairway. The clubhouse stands like a sentinel on a higher hill to the right, and golfers on its terrace have an excellent view over the entire hole. On busy golf days it was customary for a bell to be rung whenever a golfer failed to clear the water.

The Wild Coast region is known for its fickle weather, and a gentle day can suddenly turn into a stormy one. In 1984, soon after its opening, the course hosted a Sunshine Tour event that featured name players such as Seve Ballesteros and Gary Player. On the second day, tournament director Dennis Bruyns set the course up for the wind forecast from the southwest, but in the afternoon it unexpectedly switched direction, blowing at near gale-force into the faces of golfers arriving on the 18th tee. Playing off the back, they were faced with an impossible carry over the water, such was the wind's strength. To everyone's embarrassment, including that of Gary Player, ball after ball fell short of the fairway into the water. Contestants had to take a penalty drop on the ladies' tee on the other side of the water. The bell was chiming as regularly as if it had been seized by a band of campanologists.

The spectacular rolling terrain on which the American Robert Trent Jones Junior (whose father laid out Killarney in Johannesburg) designed the course lends itself to challenging tee shots like those faced at the 18th. Another, on the par-five 12th, is played off the edge of a steep plateau into a valley below, while that on the par-three 13th crosses a ravine. The uneven nature of the landscape meant Trent Jones Junior designed six par threes (par 70) to accommodate his routing plan.

The course climbs and falls over a large area of land, offering splendid views, and it has become a carts-only facility to help speed up play. The golf club, separate from the hotel and casino complex, employs colourful Xhosa women caddies who are among the best ball spotters you will find.

Although the Wild Coast Sun course, just south of Port Edward, measures only 5 800 metres, it remains a regular tournament venue on the Sunshine Tour, and Mark McNulty has won there six times. On good days, players have scored as low as 61, but it is a ferocious test when the wind gets up.

The Wild Coast Sun's par-three 13th (left) and par-four 18th (overleaf) are postcard-perfect holes on one of South Africa's most scenic courses.

THE
zulu kingdom

Champagne Sports

Prince's Grant

Victoria
Country Club

Zimbali

Cotswold Downs
DURBAN

Beachwood
Durban
Country Club

Selborne
Umdoni Park

Southbroom
San Lameer

PORT EDWARD

there are seventy golf courses to choose from in this enormous region, which can be split into four distinct parts – Durban, the South Coast, the North Coast, and the Midlands. Blessed with a tropical climate, KwaZulu-Natal is hot and humid in summer while its scenic coast provides a wonderful winter golfing destination, with idyllic golfing conditions from April to August.

The South Coast has long been a favourite with golfers, boasting a variety of charming holiday courses stretching all the way from Umkomaas to Port Edward. These are fun, shortish 18-hole layouts and are inexpensive to play. The North Coast is a new growth area that has seen the establishment of several golf estates and the development of its own international airport. The holiday resort town of Ballito has tripled in size in recent years and is now home to three estates, Zimbali, Umhlali and Simbithi, where local designer Peter Matkovich has built a unique par-60 course in the tropical forest with 13 par-three holes. In Zululand, the development of the old Eshowe Golf Club into an estate has helped boost the town.

A golfing explosion has taken place in the central to northern Drakensberg region, where the Champagne Sports Resort, long the only 18-hole course of quality in the area, has been joined by superb new courses at the Nondela (an Ernie Els design) and Dunblane (Peter Matkovich) estates.

San Lameer

COURSE DESIGNER Peter Matkovich
OPENED 1992

Several of the new courses in KwaZulu-Natal today are the work of Peter Matkovich, who lives on the Simbithi golf estate at Ballito. It all started for him at the San Lameer resort/estate near Southbroom on the South Coast in the early 1990s, where his pioneering and exciting style of design work first captured the attention of local golfers and launched a prolific career late in life.

Matkovich has been South Africa's answer to revolutionary American course architect Pete Dye in terms of introducing controversial and refreshing design features to his many projects. At San Lameer he showed imagination and initiative in fitting a fluent 18-hole course on to a hilly site that had once been home to a jungle swamp in the inhospitable tropical bush.

The result is a mix of challenging and spectacular holes, many of them involving water hazards, particularly in the low-lying areas below the clubhouse. San Lameer is a strategic course where golfers are constantly asked to take risks, yet also have safer options to explore.

With a five-star resort hotel and a wide choice of villas to rent, this is a regular tournament venue, the best known being the national finals of the annual Sanlam Cancer Challenge, played at more than 400 golf clubs around South Africa and Namibia.

San Lameer is built on a low-lying flood plain with plenty of water, and the par-four 6th (above) and 18th holes (right) require accuracy from tee to green.

Southbroom

COURSE DESIGNER Arthur Lawrence Mandy
OPENED 1948

Golf in the upmarket South Coast 'village' of Southbroom is an integral part of the community. Narrow roads wind among the unfenced holes and circle the clubhouse, where the limited number of parking spaces seems to suggest that many golfers arrive on foot or are dropped off.

The Southbroom Golf Club is everything you would expect from a holiday destination golf course – fun and flattering to play, short yet deceptively challenging in its shot values, and popular in the holidays when it is packed with golfers from sunrise to sunset. They appreciate both its top-class conditioning and the friendly welcome in the clubhouse.

The course is one of those that typically evolve over the years with input from passionate club members, several of whom have devoted themselves to improving Southbroom. The original design was by AL Mandy, a notable Natal golfer in the 1920s, who turned his attention to green-keeping and course architecture. It has stood the test of time, although he would hardly recognise it today after many additions and alterations.

Some notably attractive and uniquely designed holes give Southbroom a special quality above other South Coast courses.

Southbroom's par-three 4th (above) and par-three 8th (below) are part of a quaint, well-conditioned coastal course.

Umdoni Park

COURSE DESIGNER Sid Brews
OPENED 1930

In the coastal forest at Umdoni Park is the 17th hole, a long uphill par four. It is named Tiger, after a nineteenth-century incident when Richard Pennington was mauled here by a wounded leopard (often called a tiger at that time). Other holes have names that convey a sense of history – Majuba, Dick King, Delville Wood – while the Botha House hole adjoins the stately seafront home built for General Louis Botha when he was Prime Minister.

Not long ago Umdoni Park was a hidden gem. Significant improvements to the old course, the development of Selborne golf estate nearby, and easier accessibility from the village of Pennington next door have attracted a growing number of golfers to its scenic and old-fashioned charms. It offers mostly seaside golf on undulating slopes overlooking the ocean, but also ventures into the magnificent indigenous forest that covers this nature reserve bequeathed to the nation by Sir Frank Reynolds. His original home Lynton Hall, opposite Selborne, is a luxury hotel.

Umdoni Park has a quaint colonial clubhouse, a short course at 5 572 metres and an eccentric collection of holes, but is a fabulous place to escape for golf of a challenging nature.

The par-three 16th (above) and the par-five 18th (below) at Umdoni Park both have elevated tees with magnificent ocean views.

Selborne

COURSE DESIGNER Denis Barker
OPENED 1987

Selborne is where modern golf course living as we know it originated in South Africa. Yet it was not the creation of a property developer but of a wealthy South Coast dairy farmer, Denis Barker, who was prescient enough to glimpse the future of golf on a visit he made to the United States.

Barker noted the luxury homes set back from the fairways of many American courses he played, and decided that his farm along the N2 highway near Pennington on the South Coast would be ideally suited for a golf estate. He was ahead of his time by a few years. When Gary Player declined the offer to design the course, Barker embarked on the entire project himself.

The result is a surprisingly good course for a layman designer on difficult rolling terrain, although it is a relatively easy walk on an attractive low-density estate that owes much to Barker's early vision. As both the original owner and developer he could set his own parameters. He did not want the homes to determine the routing or intrude on the golfing experience at Selborne, so they are mostly hidden away in the forest on the front nine, and blend in naturally elsewhere. With its magnificent trees and water features, the estate resembles a leafy botanical park, with abundant wildlife.

Selborne is a thirty-minute drive south on the N2 from Durban Airport, and has become a popular golf resort, with access to nearby beaches. Barker's old manor house is part of the hotel complex. Umdoni Park Golf Club is just a few minutes away.

Many golfers underestimate Selborne, judging it to be on the short side even from the back tees, but the uneven nature of the holes, the proximity of the bush, and some sloping greens make it a tricky layout on which to score well. Not being an experienced course architect or a low-handicap golfer, Barker designed a course he and his golfing friends could enjoy playing for the rest of their lives. It therefore contains half-a-dozen short par fours where accuracy and strategy are key tactics, and where the long hitters must take risks to force a birdie.

A pleasant aspect of Selborne is the brisk pace of play. The back of the scorecard tells of the local golf lore, which puts emphasis on etiquette and consideration for other fourballs – all aspects of the game Barker cherished during his time there.

The strategic par-four 18th hole typifies the Selborne golfing experience.

Durban Country Club

COURSE DESIGNERS Laurie Waters/George Waterman
OPENED 1922

Durban Country Club, our equivalent of St Andrews, has always enjoyed reverential status among older golfers in South Africa. For many years it was considered the premier course and leading championship layout. Yet for half a century a dark cloud hung overhead, with the future of the golf course threatened by Durban city councillors who wanted the valuable land bulldozed so it could be turned into a profitable development.

Durban CC was the first truly classic golf course designed and built in South Africa, in the mould of the great links of Scotland and England. It was the forerunner of early masterpieces such as Maccauvlei, East London, Humewood and the East course at Royal Johannesburg & Kensington.

In 1922, the year the layout was constructed by George Waterman, with design input from Laurie Waters, the standard of courses around the Union was poor. The tendency had been to situate them on flat and featureless sites because these were the cheapest to lease and easiest to build on. No earthmoving was required, and golfers did not seem bothered about aesthetics.

The Durban Golf Club course at Greyville, for example, had been built on a low-lying swampy vlei prone to flooding, and the questionable quality of golf there persuaded members that it would be in the city's best interests to build another, better course elsewhere. Durban GC had become an unreliable venue for hosting the South African Championships, and an alternative course was needed before they returned to Durban in 1924.

The backers of the new club found a desirable location in the Umgeni flats, a swampland edged by giant sand dunes, and the land was leased from the town council. From the start it proved an unhappy partnership, one that was to concern the club in the decades ahead. The threat of the lease suddenly being terminated was a real possibility from the 1950s onwards. Durban CC even acquired land at Umhlanga Rocks in case the course was closed. And because the club was originally unable to secure all the land it required, the course is today a virtual island surrounded by busy motorways and roads, instead of enjoying an unspoilt, natural link to the beach.

There are few holes in the country as well known as Durban Country Club's par-five 3rd.

It resembled a links when first opened for play — an out-and-back routing, holes rolling over the dunes, sandy wastelands everywhere, and some formidable bunkers. Gradually, however, the fairways became defined by tropical bush and tall casuarina trees, most of which were only recently felled. Over the years, as the conditioning and manicuring improved, it took on more of a parkland appearance.

The course is famous for its opening five holes in the dunes facing the seafront, and the par-five 3rd has in its time been ranked among the 18 greatest holes in the world. Played from a high tee into a narrow valley, it is stunning in every respect, the fairway rising towards a narrow green. The 1st is a tricky par four with one of the more interestingly designed greens. The 2nd and 4th are par threes in opposite directions, played from elevated tees, but different in character. The 5th is a great championship par four, again from a tee set high in the dunes, to an offset plateau fairway.

Had the design maintained a constant flow of undulating holes it might today be considered one of the world's great courses, but critics contend that several holes on flat terrain furthest from the clubhouse contrast poorly with those preceding them. Yet there are sublime exceptions, like the par-five 8th, with its green perched on top of a dune, and the par-four 17th, its fairway rippling in a series of hollows to a raised green.

Two holes define the indescribable charm of Durban CC. First is the par-three 12th with a green built on a narrow dune, falling away steeply on each side. It is known as the Prince of Wales after the club's first royal visitor took seventeen shots there on a 1925 visit. Second is the short par-four 18th, just 250 metres and mocked by some as insignificant, but a memorable conclusion to the round, offering various options off the tee. The green can be driven, but the humpback fairway is narrow, and problems abound on either side. Framed behind the green is the white-gabled clubhouse, a sight as distinctive for South African golfers as the Royal & Ancient clubhouse on the Old Course.

As many as sixteen South African Opens have been hosted here since the first in 1924, some memorable championships among them, like in 1928 when Jock Brews made an eagle two at the last to win. Gary Player won three of his thirteen Opens at Durban CC, and Sid Brews had six Open triumphs between 1925 and 1934 while serving as the club pro. John Bland has the course and Open record, a 10-under-par 62 in the opening round in 1994. At its peak in 1993 the club had 11 592 members.

Durban North and the beachfront form the backdrop to the par-three 2nd hole at Durban Country Club, one of the country's premier championship layouts.

Beachwood

COURSE DESIGNERS Sid Brews/Gary Player
OPENED 1930

Golf courses do not get much closer to the ocean than Beachwood, where you can literally pitch a shot off the practice putting area on to the white sandy beach that stretches the length of the layout. Situated on a narrow strip of coastal forest and mangrove swamp midway between Durban and Umhlanga Rocks, it is a wonderful challenge for golfers wanting to know how straight they can hit the ball.

Beachwood is nowadays Durban Country Club's second golf course, the two clubs having amalgamated due to common interests in 1994. Durban CC had for many years been interested in acquiring another 18 holes, and Beachwood could not have been a better fit. It was close by, and the two courses are similar in several respects, built on low-lying sandy dunes.

A stylish new clubhouse was constructed, and Gary Player was called in to upgrade the Beachwood course, which, while attractive in its sandy setting, had deteriorated in quality. Some will have mourned the loss of the old course's ruggedly natural beauty, but the redesign modernised the layout, with strikingly shaped new greens and bunkering bringing it up to the level of Durban CC itself. In fact, there have been times when the adopted sibling has outshone the original course in looks and conditioning.

Unlike the Durban course, the Beachwood course is tucked away in a more private and leafy part of Durban North, with a quiet access road. Playing there is not only a tranquil experience by comparison, but a memorable one. The only disturbances come from the light aircraft that fly overhead, particularly as they glide in low over the par-five 17th fairway before landing at Virginia Airport. Attractive homes line the inland side of the course on a higher terrace.

Beachwood is not a course for the novice. Several of its holes are downright intimidating to play, bordered as they are by the natural bush and the swamp on the front nine. Subtle changes in elevation make for great sightlines from the back tees of virtually every hole. Nothing is hidden from you, and that includes all the trouble.

Durban CC finishes with a short par four, and Beachwood is also unusual in having a 185-metre par three as the 18th, ending in front of the clubhouse.

The green of the short par-three 2nd (above) lies next to mangrove swamps. The par-three 12th and the par-five 17th (right) run next to each other and share a fairway.

Prince's Grant

COURSE DESIGNER Peter Matkovich
OPENED 1994

Prince's Grant stands apart from many of the modern golf estate developments in the way it respects and upholds the finer traditions of the game. This secluded hideaway resort on the KwaZulu-Natal North Coast has a clubhouse that reeks of golf: walls crammed with old photographs, paintings and memorabilia, and comfortable upstairs accommodation where golfers can stay close to the game.

The clubhouse architecture is old-style American colonial, similar to that at Shinnecock Hills on Long Island, and the distinctive structure stands on a ridge overlooking the opening holes of the course. Prince's Grant was conceived by developer Guy Smith, who has a passion for the game's traditional values and dislikes artificial modern contrivances. One exception is the golf carts many use to play the hilly layout, although walking is still encouraged.

Smith has since developed another similar experience at Gowrie Farm in the KwaZulu-Natal Midlands, nearer to his home in Pietermaritzburg, where he designed the 9-hole course using traditional old-fashioned construction methods. Both places have an appealing remoteness about them.

One of the Prince's Grant traditions is a 72-hole strokeplay tournament to which sixty of the country's best amateurs are invited each January, and where the SA Amateur champion is honoured at a dinner and given membership.

While initially there was universal praise for the Matkovich-designed course, the estate took several years to get off the ground. It is just an hour's drive north from Durban and most stands were bought for holiday homes, so very little building took place during the 1990s. However, Prince's Grant boomed in the new millennium, and it has become a sought-after weekend escape.

Built on former sugarcane land adjoining the ocean, the course has a great mix of holes, where you play through valleys, across the tops of ridges, and venture close to the sea and a lagoon. The remaining coastal forest on the property also comes into play on the back nine after starting out on two holes, 10 and 11, that are links-like in their shaping and appearance.

Prince's Grant has a wonderful finishing stretch. Number 14 traverses a high ridge, and the par-five 15th plummets spectacularly downhill from its high tee, with magnificent views of the coastline. That is followed by a short par four next to the lagoon, a tricky par three, and another par five to end.

Prince's Grant has Scottish heritage in the links features of its par-four 10th hole (left). Fever trees are reflected in the water hazard of the par-five 6th hole (overleaf).

Zimbali

COURSE DESIGNER Tom Weiskopf
OPENED 1998

Zimbali is a luxury resort development on the Dolphin Coast outside Ballito. Its 18-hole course, designed by the American Tom Weiskopf – a talented major champion and course architect – has a similarly opulent look, having matured into a lush creation.

Weiskopf has been a prolific although low-key course designer since retiring from tournament golf, but with a limited international portfolio. He has designed only two courses outside the United States: Zimbali and the famous Loch Lomond layout in Scotland. At first glance they would not seem to have much in common, apart from excellent reputations and innovative design work, yet they both traverse forests and have significant water features.

Zimbali originally appeared as a course of two distinct halves, the exposed front nine in open rolling terrain on former sugarcane fields and the secluded back nine in the dense coastal forest. Now, however, it has a more harmonious flow due to the growth of both the housing estate and the foliage defining the layout. The balance of the holes is much more apparent.

Significantly helping to attain that flow from one nine to the next has been the closure of the busy arterial coastal road that divided the estate and the course in half. A new road has been built further inland.

Continuously undulating, and built on several levels to allow for steep changes in elevation, with significant gaps between green and tee, Zimbali is a carts-only course in true resort style. You climb from the difficult par-four 15th on the valley floor of the coastal forest right up to the high 18th with its ocean views, a fierce finishing par four that encapsulates Weiskopf's old-school design thinking. Famous as a player for his pure striking of long irons, he prefers a closing hole that rewards more skilful golfers if they can produce two of their best shots of the day, rather than the compromise par-five holes so prevalent on modern layouts.

The elegant and luxurious clubhouse, hidden and shaded in the forest above the 18th green, is a veritable oasis at the end of a round.

The Zimbali Coastal Resort itself is expanding and emerging as a premier destination through a joint venture partnership between Tongaat-Hulett Developments and IFA Hotels & Resorts (Kuwait). Zimbali will soon have a second golf course, The Lakes, to be designed by Gary Player.

The par-four 18th hole at Zimbali has all the hallmarks of a great finishing hole.

Zimbali is a well-rounded course with a variety of holes that provide a thorough test of the game. Clockwise from top left: the par-five 12th requires some long hitting, while both the par-four 2nd and par-three 11th require placement off the tee.

Cotswold Downs

COURSE DESIGNER Peter Matkovich
OPENED 2006

The wonders of modern golf course construction methods, and the versatility of the golf cart, made it possible to build this expansive estate layout on the rolling terrain of Hillcrest outside Durban. Cotswold Downs covers a vast area of land, many of its holes situated on two separate hilltops, and others in the surrounding valleys.

Peter Matkovich had a big budget to work with and the freedom to route the holes as he wished. The result is a memorable design that flows quite superbly from the very first hole to the last among indigenous vegetation that has replaced sugarcane plantations. Its setting evokes reminders of the old Circle Country Club layout, now closed, which lay in hills not far from here.

Because of the undulating topography – carts are essential to get around – there is no shortage of dramatic holes. They begin with the 1st, a superb par five with a prominent tree guarding the approach to the green, and continue to the finishing hole, an even more challenging par five bordered by a wetland area. The elevation changes have been handled well in terms of the design. A 'parachute drop' par three, the 5th, has a staggeringly high tee above the green, while the par-four 17th falls spectacularly down the slopes of a hill.

The par-four 6th (above) and the par-four 4th (right) are both superb holes built on hilly terrain, while the par-five 1st hole (overleaf) plays around a prominent fig tree.

Victoria Country Club

COURSE DESIGNER Bob Grimsdell
OPENED 1933

Majestic parkland golf is on offer at this Pietermaritzburg venue on the slopes of Town Hill, where an early Grimsdell layout has been modernised by the Golf Data design and construction team. It re-opened for play in 2007 as part of a golf estate that happily does not intrude much into the course.

Victoria Country Club has benefited from new greens, while a tree-removal campaign opened up other holes and allowed more hours of sunshine on to greens that previously struggled to grow in the shade of massive trees.

Golf was first played in Pietermaritzburg in 1886, with the formation of Maritzburg Golf Club just seven years after the great battle of Isandhlwana not far to the north. Victoria CC also has a long history. After more than sixty years as Maritzburg Country Club, it merged in 1996 with the downtown Victoria Club (founded in 1859) to become Victoria CC.

Victoria CC is a course of contrastingly long and short par fours, elevation changes and sloping fairways. It hosted the 1989 SA Amateur Championship, where Ernie Els won the 72-hole strokeplay title, then lost the matchplay final in a titanic struggle against Craig Rivett that went 38 holes before being decided.

The long uphill par-four 14th (above) and the par-five 11th (right) are feature holes on a well-designed course built on a hillside.

Champagne Sports

COURSE DESIGNER Hugh Baiocchi
OPENED 1999

The golf clubhouse at Champagne Sports Resort is set on a high bluff overlooking the course. It has impressive views towards the Drakensberg mountain range, including the distant twin peaks of Champagne Castle and Cathkin Peak.

The course opens with one of the longest holes in South Africa. To reach the back tee of this 605-metre par five you must climb back uphill, passing through a memorial garden, to a spot seldom frequented by visiting golfers. There is a 110-metre difference between this and the more popular club tee in the valley below, but it is a spectacular height from which to launch a drive in the crisp mountain air over a river to the fairway below. If you are walking, it takes about ten minutes before you get to your ball for the second shot.

Extreme changes in elevation are part of the challenge at this central Drakensberg resort. The 2nd is a stunning long par four with the tee set high above the river on the left, presenting a challenging carry to an angled fairway that falls precipitously to the green. An exhausting climb up the steep 3rd is rewarded with the glorious par-three 4th, played from a high tee to a green in another valley below, dauntingly fronted by a water hazard.

The course continues to undulate back and forth, but in slightly more sedate fashion, before virtually flattening out on the less dramatic and more conventional back nine. Yet it remains competitive throughout, with an interesting trio of holes to finish – a long par three and two solid par fours.

Golf of this stature and quality of conditioning is a relatively new experience in the Drakensberg, where for many years the courses were predominantly of the shortish 9-hole variety like neighbouring Monks Cowl, its fairways firm and fast in the winter months. Champagne Sports, which graduated from a 9-holer in the late 1990s to a 6 700-metre layout, has kikuyu fairways and bent grass greens that retain their colour all year, even if the surroundings turn brown after the first frosts – making it both a summer and winter golfing destination. There is an outside deck at the clubhouse where golfers can relax in summer, and a fireplace inside for winter.

The majesty of the Drakensberg is in full view at Champagne Sports Resort's par-three 4th hole (right) and par-four 18th (overleaf).

THE bushveld & kalahari

   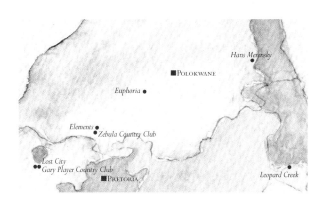

bushveld golf courses are unique to the African continent, yet they are a relatively recent phenomenon in South Africa, where they were few and far between until the beginning of this new millennium.

Customarily set in arid indigenous bush, these courses are primarily in the north of the country – in North West Province, Mpumalanga and Limpopo. One notable exception is the mine course jewel of Sishen, set in a camelthorn forest on the edge of the Kalahari Desert in the Northern Cape. Bushveld courses have been mushrooming in Limpopo in particular, where remotely situated golf estates embracing wilderness areas and wild game have become popular in the malaria-free Waterberg region. The presence of wildlife and birdlife – the sights and sounds of the bush – is part of the charm of most bushveld and Kalahari courses.

One of the original bushveld courses is Hans Merensky, adjoining the Kruger National Park, where herds of wild animals had to be driven away during its construction in the 1960s. There is even a course within the park itself, a 9-hole layout near Skukuza camp, once restricted to park staff but now open to visitors. The 1st tee carries a warning that wild animals may be encountered during a round. Two of South Africa's best championship courses, the Gary Player at Sun City and Leopard Creek on the southern boundary of the Kruger National Park, also provide some memorable bushveld golfing experiences.

Euphoria

COURSE DESIGNER Annika Sorenstam
OPENED 2008

Getting the world's former No. 1 woman golfer to design her first course in South Africa was a marketing coup for this Limpopo resort hydro/estate, roughly midway between Pretoria and Polokwane. Her image is proudly displayed in and around an estate of nearly 800 homes.

Annika Sorenstam was not too active on the design front during her playing career, so it is exceptional to have a course in South Africa with her name attached to it. Her association with Euphoria was put together by the International Management Group (IMG). They assign star clients to course design projects undertaken by their design arm, European Golf Design, a joint venture with the European Tour.

Euphoria is a big, testing championship layout, and even though it is on a relatively flat piece of land you still need a golf cart to get around in comfort, such are the distances between holes. It is located in bushveld, but the undulating nature of the fairways, the distinctive and prominent bunkering, and the long, wavy native grasses in the rough convey a links-like look in places.

A feature of Euphoria is the cableway that links the clubhouse to a restaurant and viewing deck built high on a hill overlooking the course – a perfect place to relax and take in the sights at the end of the day.

Euphoria's par-four 16th (above) and par-five 9th (right) show the natural grasses and beautiful greens on this strategic layout.

Hans Merensky

COURSE DESIGNER Bob Grimsdell
OPENED 1967

The fame of this bushveld course in the northeastern Limpopo mining and tourism town of Phalaborwa has everything to do with the wildlife that abounds on its fairways. Bordering the fence of the Kruger National Park, it has been host to every member of the animal kingdom's Big Five.

This is golf in the wild with a capital W, because a round at Hans Merensky is like stepping out of your car in the park itself, and going for a wander in the bush. On some occasions you might not see anything other than a few impala, baboons or warthogs, but there are times when a giraffe will quietly stroll out of the trees behind you. Golfers have spotted rare kills by leopard and cheetah on the course, and a buffalo once charged the green-keeper's pick-up truck. Tragically, a golfer from Germany was killed by an enraged elephant in 1998 when she became curious about the animal's proximity in the bush adjoining one of the holes, and ventured too close in order to take photographs of it.

Danger does lurk on the fairways, but security on this resort and housing estate is tight. Any report of big cats means golfers must retreat to the clubhouse. Regulars do not worry about the hippos and crocodiles that inhabit the water hazards, although no one ventures out after dark when the hippos march along the fairways in search of grazing.

This land used to be part of the Kruger National Park until a deal was struck in the mid-1960s between the then Parks Board and the Palabora Mining Company, South Africa's only producer of refined copper. Building the course was a considerable undertaking: it had to be routed through thick bushveld, with beaters first driving animals away from the area, and constantly having to flee for their lives. It was named after the late Dr Hans Merensky, an eminent geologist who in 1912 discovered the 'hill of copper' that has enriched the region. The original clubhouse was one of the largest buildings under thatch in Africa.

The undulating course, a relatively old-fashioned design by today's standards, though interestingly varied with terrific par threes, was not that well known until the mining company decided to make it part of the Sunshine Tour. Seven tournaments were held between 1985 and 1991, attracting all the top players, and the course's reputation spread quickly as a result.

A group of resident giraffe moves between the holes at Hans Merensky, seen here on the par-five 16th (right). Hippos and crocodiles can be spotted in the dam on the par-three 8th (overleaf).

Leopard Creek

COURSE DESIGNER Gary Player
OPENED 1996

The sluggishly flowing brown water of the Crocodile River marks the southern boundary of the Kruger National Park. Near Malelane Gate it is all that separates this vast wilderness from the lush Eden that is the Leopard Creek golf estate. South Africa's top-ranked golf course occupies a remarkable site that offers a stunning contrast between two diverse worlds.

It is rare to find a course that meets expectations as much as Leopard Creek does in terms of its remoteness and isolation, its proximity to wildlife, and the beauty of its surroundings. A thatch-roofed colonial-style clubhouse close to the river adds to the experience of being swept up into a captivating African place. On the golf course side it overlooks a large water hazard, towards which the closing holes sweep side by side down a hill to their respective greens. From the upper rear deck you have views across the river to the park, with its vast expanse of grasslands and bush.

An even more magical moment comes when you arrive at the green of the par-five 13th hole. Built at great expense, it sits high on a bluff directly over the river, giving an uninterrupted sightline of the wilderness on the other side. From here, it is not uncommon to see hippos bathing below or a herd of elephants shuffling through the park. And there are few golfing venues in the world where you can stand on the elevated 18th tee, looking down on the clubhouse in the valley below, and watch giraffe loping across the fairway. It is rare to see animals on the course during the day, yet they do come and go from the park, and residents are warned not to venture out on the fairways at night.

Leopard Creek was the inspiration and dream golfing locale of wealthy South African businessman (chief executive of Richemont) and golfing philanthropist Johann Rupert. He converted this bushveld property near the Mozambique border into one of the great golfing challenges, utilising the design expertise of both Gary Player and Jack Nicklaus, and combined it with a visually enchanting feast of nature.

The course has been refined and altered over the years, improving the look and playability of the 18 holes, so that today it merges seamlessly into the surrounding landscape. Player was the original designer, but some years later Nicklaus, who owns a house on the course, provided input of his own with a few design tweaks.

Leopard Creek has one of the most thrilling risk-and-reward closing par fives.

Leopard Creek is an exclusive private club for members and their guests, but opportunity to play the course is open to visiting golfers staying at a selection of wildlife lodges close by, who have to pay the club a high-end green fee. Despite its remoteness – a four-hour drive from Johannesburg – the course is usually busy at weekends, with members staying at their properties on the estate. The houses are generally hidden from view along the riverbank or in the thick bush. Rupert has reduced the number of dwellings originally proposed, not wishing to disturb the environment further.

This is a hot, humid region, and the climate is at its most pleasant in the winter months, when game viewing in the park is also more rewarding. The high-ceilinged clubhouse is a cool retreat after golf, its décor paying homage to the great traditional clubhouses of Britain and America, with rooms that evoke historic eras in the game. Rupert based his founders' locker room upstairs on that at Seminole in Florida.

In a climate of simmering temperatures, it is astonishing to find such outstanding conditioning from tee to green, a mix of kikuyu fairways and bent grass greens. Rupert has spared no expense in ensuring that the manicuring of the course, plus the quick pace of the greens, is up to the highest standards he has experienced in his travels around the world.

A fascinating feature is the striking life-sized statue of a leopard on every hole. Sculptor Dylan Lewis created them to capture the graceful animal's different poses, quiet and restful on the opening holes, and then energetically in pursuit of a buck on the back nine. It finally gets a grasp of its prey on the 16th tee, where by now the course is also beginning to take big chunks out of the golfers.

Rupert hosts the Alfred Dunhill Championship at Leopard Creek each year. The course is a challenge for the best, having a superb variety of risk-and-reward holes, including three par fives on the back nine where water comes into play, some of these hazards being home to hippos and crocodiles. One hole that makes spellbinding viewing is the downhill par-five 18th with its island green. It has been the scene of many a dramatic finish to the tournament, none more so than in 2007 when Ernie Els put two balls in the water around the green on the final day, taking a triple-bogey 8 that cost him the title by one shot.

A Dylan Lewis sculpture of a leopard decorates each tee at Leopard Creek, such as this one looking out over the par-three 5th.

Zebula
Country Club

COURSE DESIGNER Peter Matkovich
OPENED 2004

The Waterberg is an attractive bushveld region, characterised by rolling hills, mountain escarpments and abundant wildlife. Its relative closeness to the Gauteng metropolitan area and its malaria-free climate have made it an ideal getaway for city dwellers. Zebula's American owner Steve Dunn first conceptualised the combination of 'golf meeting game' on a 1 200-hectare resort estate two hours' drive from Johannesburg.

Zebula is wonderfully remote. You leave the spa town of Bela-Bela and venture on to dirt roads, where you capture the real aroma of the Waterberg. There is little sign of habitation along the way. Once you are inside the estate, a single-track road leads through quiet leafy bush for several kilometres before reaching the lodge and golf course. Homes are scattered about the property. It is five-star accommodation, with a spa and superb practice facilities.

The course is flat and easy to walk. Wide fairways framed by bushveld trees add to the character of the design, challenging yet player-friendly. Various species of buck roam the property, and the Big Five are next door at Mabalingwe Game Reserve.

Zebula was built in open grassland below the Waterberg where plains game roam free. The 16th (above) and 3rd holes (right) are both superb par fours.

Elements

COURSE DESIGNER Peter Matkovich
OPENED 2005

Rainfall is never reliable in the Waterberg, and this hilly region can go months without any significant rain to quench the earth. It is a dry, hot part of the country mostly suitable for game farms, yet an increasing number of golf estates – those with plentiful water resources – have also become part of the landscape.

Although Elements is close to Zebula, where Peter Matkovich designed his first Waterberg course, they are very different to look at, due to the changing nature of the terrain. Whereas Zebula is a spacious, flat layout on open plains, Elements lies inside a rugged and rocky valley between low hills. Matkovich, enamoured by the beauty and potential of the site, felt that only an expansive championship layout was suitable to complement this land.

The result is a demanding golf course that poses tough challenges throughout its 18 holes. The classic bushveld design has infinite variety as it rolls through the heavily treed landscape, even if there is a preponderance of right-to-left shaped holes. Starting with the unusual 1st hole, an uphill par four where the approach shot needs to traverse a narrow gap in the bush, you know you are in for a test.

Having left clouds of dust trailing behind you on the dirt road from Bela-Bela, you will be fascinated by the lushness of the Elements course against the harsh African backdrop. It is superbly conditioned and manicured, up to the quality of any parkland course in Gauteng. Water features are not prominent, but it pays not to stray from the closely mown areas – elsewhere is rough country.

A stream runs through part of the course to a big dam in the lowest point of the valley that is the focal point of the two closing holes on each nine. The clubhouse is built on a ridge and overlooks the dam, which was an empty, deep hole in the ground when the course was being built. Fortunately, good rains filled it up and created a magical setting.

The many big trees lining the holes are an integral part of the challenge, testing a golfer's shot-making skills. Many individual holes are memorable. The 9th is an excellent par three with an uninterrupted water hazard all the way from tee to green, while the 18th is a steeply downhill par five approaching from the opposite direction, water guarding the left of its green – a great risk-and-reward finishing challenge.

The 8th, 9th and 18th holes all centre on this water feature below the clubhouse (left). The par-five 7th (overleaf) shows how each fairway is separated by indigenous bush.

Lost City

COURSE DESIGNER Gary Player
OPENED 1993

Golf enjoyed a boom in popularity in South Africa in the early 1990s, so it was only a matter of time before a second course was built at the busy Sun City resort in North West Province, and this coincided with the development of its Palace of the Lost City complex. Hotel magnate Sol Kerzner briefed Gary Player to create something that would be grand enough to complement his opulent new hotel. Player pulled out all the stops, and the Lost City was a significantly spectacular layout from the start.

Not only was it separate from the Gary Player Country Club (GPCC) in an adjoining Pilanesberg valley, but it was radically different in design and theme. Whereas the GPCC had a South African bushveld feel, Player created a rugged look at Lost City, resembling courses built in the Arizona desert. Waste bunkers filled with native grasses and desert plants were part of the setting.

Also in keeping with the American resort course theme was the decision to make Lost City a carts-only course. Player routed his layout with that in mind, taking tees high up on the slopes of two steep hills to create wonderful elevations. It was the first course to adopt this policy in South Africa, the golfing community at that time being mostly walkers. Lost City's hilly terrain, and long distances between greens and tees, made carts essential in the valley heat.

South Africa was moving towards a new government in the early 1990s, and the Lost City experience was all about attracting foreign tourists to the resort. Player created a unique hazard at Lost City that immediately put the course on the map internationally. A large pit was built on the edge of the par-three 13th green and filled with dozens of crocodiles. It became known as one of the most dangerous holes in golf, even though the only possible danger would be if you attempted to retrieve your ball from this area. Sunshine Tour professional Graeme Francis did exactly that in a tournament at Lost City, leaping into the pit and playing a recovery shot. He was disqualified for his trouble.

A special course like this required a novel clubhouse. Lost City's clubhouse is surely one of the best in the world, its stone boulders producing a building intended to recreate what Great Zimbabwe must have looked like before it became the Zimbabwe Ruins. The clubhouse stands on a ridge overlooking the 9th and 18th holes, their fairways curving around one large water hazard.

The par-four 17th hole depicts the wonderful topography of the course and surrounds.

Lost City's resort-style course has some sensational holes. Clockwise from top left: the attractive par-four 1st; the par-three 13th with a water hazard that is home to crocodiles; and the two incoming holes that are in full view from the clubhouse.

Gary Player
Country Club

COURSE DESIGNER Gary Player
OPENED 1979

This is not just one of South Africa's greatest championship courses, but an iconic showplace that has been pivotal in changing the golfing landscape in this country over three decades. It has had a substantial influence in the growth of the game here, helping transform South Africa into one of the world's foremost golfing nations.

The Gary Player Country Club (GPCC) is part of the glitzy Sun City resort next to the Pilanesberg Game Reserve, and for eleven months of the year is available for the use of its guests and day visitors. But it was built first and foremost as a major tournament venue rather than as a fun resort layout. In the year it opened for play, it hosted the Sun City Classic on the Sunshine Tour, which Player won to put the official seal of approval on its worthiness to test the best. Since then the resort has hosted more than fifty professional tournaments, including the Women's World Cup, and quite a few amateur world championships.

The GPCC had the reputation of being the longest course in Africa and by far the toughest challenge. It may no longer be No. 1 in overall length, but its difficulty remains unsurpassed. There should be a warning notice about that on the pathway to the 1st tee. The average golfer is advised to play off forward tees to best enjoy the round, but the GPCC tends to bring out the macho element in golfers, who want to claim afterwards that they have tested themselves off the tips.

The course, and Sun City, became instantly famous worldwide and caught the imagination of golfers everywhere when its developer and hotel magnate Sol Kerzner conceived the idea of the first million-dollar golf tournament in December 1981. Five of the biggest names in golf – Jack Nicklaus, Gary Player, Lee Trevino, Seve Ballesteros and Johnny Miller – accepted invitations to the first tournament. It proved an immediate hit, with Miller beating Ballesteros in a memorable 9-hole play-off to win $500 000, a mind-boggling sum in golf at the time. The leading money-winner on the PGA Tour in America that year earned $375 000.

Two young warthogs frolic on the apron of the par-three 16th hole.

147

The Million Dollar Challenge was born, and has been played every year since – an enduring monument to Kerzner's belief that anything was possible at Sun City. The field grew to ten players the second year (currently twelve), and in 1987 there was a winner-take-all tournament where Ian Woosnam became the first man in golf to walk off with $1 million. The other players hated being left empty-handed, so the following year the purse was raised to $1.65 million, with the last man getting $50 000. The champion continued to receive $1 million until the year 2000, when the first prize was doubled to $2 million to reflect changing financial fortunes. Several other tournaments were offering more than a million, so Sun City upped the ante, but reverted to $1.2 million after three years.

The tournament exposed South Africans to the game's greatest in the flesh, just a two-hour drive from Johannesburg. It also revolutionised the game here at a time when 1980s sanctions were crippling sports like rugby and cricket. The tournament was televised and became a national end-of-year sporting institution. Young boys wanted to play golf, and South Africa went from having one golfing hero, Player, to producing four major champions in subsequent decades. Seven players from southern Africa have won the Million Dollar (known as the Nedbank Challenge since 2000), including three victories each by David Frost, Nick Price and Ernie Els.

The course has matured into a magnificently conditioned and thickly forested bushveld layout, its natural beauty retained because no development has taken place around its perimeter. It is bordered mainly by the hills of the Pilanesberg reserve, while Sun City hotels overlook only the closing holes. It has been upgraded and improved, but remains essentially faithful to the original design, apart from the par-four 17th, where the green was moved to the edge of the lake that serves as the resort's watersports venue.

The greens were designed in a cloverleaf shape, so the flagsticks can be placed in smaller shelves protected by greenside bunkers. Subtle slopes see golfers face lots of fast downhill putts.

There are many demanding holes, the most famous and challenging being the par-five 9th, with a large island green surrounded by rocks and water in front of the clubhouse. It commands some of the biggest crowds during the Nedbank Challenge, as the professionals are encouraged to risk going for the green with their approach shots from way back on the fairway.

The par-four 18th is also challenging, although not as much for the professionals as for the average resort player, who has a water hazard to cross for the second shot. Grandstands surround the green during the Nedbank Challenge, creating a wonderful atmosphere when filled to capacity.

The Gary Player Country Club's par-five 9th is an iconic hole of the South African golf landscape.

Sishen

COURSE DESIGNER Bob Grimsdell
OPENED 1979

Situated on the eastern edge of the Kalahari Desert, Sishen is the remotest great course in South Africa, and was the final design of respected golf course architect Bob Grimsdell before he died. He did not see his work completed.

It is a gem in the Northern Cape mining community of Kathu, threading through a protected kameeldoring (camelthorn) forest — a beautiful tree indigenous to the Kalahari. The town was established in the 1970s to provide more pleasant living conditions away from the opencast iron mines and ore dumps at nearby Sishen.

The golf club, now owned by Kumba Iron Ore, was initially meant to have 9 holes. Solly Watson, the mine manager in the 1970s, was given a budget of R250 000 for a course, but felt the proposed site would do greater justice to 18 holes, even if the club would not have a big enough membership to support it. He asked Grimsdell to create something special, and ended up spending R1.5-million. It was a wonderful investment. Over the years the club has hosted numerous tournaments, including the old Kalahari Classic on the Sunshine Tour, and also produced the 1987 SA Amateur champion Ben Fouchee.

Sishen is not a desert course as you would expect, but bushveld, and its lush appearance surprises the first-time visitor. Water hazards guard the 9th and 18th greens. There is such a peaceful aura about the course that on a still day it is possible to hear the sound of a golf ball spinning through the air. There have been recent improvements tied in with an adjoining estate development: a new clubhouse and irrigation system, and bent grass greens.

The challenge of the layout lies in the strategic positioning of the trees lining the fairways. Virtually every tee shot has to be placed correctly to have an unimpeded line to the flag. The trees are so dense that the old golfing adage that trees are ninety per cent air does not apply. The ball reacts as if it was hit against a brick wall. The kameeldoring trees have grown to immense heights because of a plentiful supply of water from the mine. The origin of their name has nothing to do with camels, but rather the giraffe. The Afrikaans word for giraffe is *kameelperd*, and the tree's old botanical name was *Acacia giraffae* (now *erioloba*). The hard, dense wood makes for perfect firewood, but it is a protected species so you need a permit to sell it.

Sishen's par-five 11th (left) and par-five 6th holes (overleaf) illustrate the challenge that camelthorn trees pose on this unique course.

THE highveld

a superb selection of terrific parkland golf courses and a sublime summer climate make the Highveld an attractive destination for golfers. And in the rarefied air the ball goes much further than it does at the coast, at least 10 metres longer with every club. Wind-free weather and warm sunny days make this a golfer's paradise for nine months of the year (September to May), while regular rainfall keeps the courses in mint condition throughout the summer. The clubs welcome visitors, and the only problem is avoiding the late-afternoon thunderstorms that are a feature of the region, where lightning strikes are a danger to anyone out on a golf course.

Golf was first played in Johannesburg in 1890, and many of the older clubs are in the suburbs immediately north of the City of Gold, including Royal Johannesburg & Kensington, Houghton – where a new course by Jack Nicklaus has replaced the old layout – Parkview, Observatory and Killarney. The game also spread east and west to the mining areas, where clubs like Germiston and ERPM have rich histories. The three biggest clubs are Royal, Country Club Johannesburg and Randpark, each with 36-hole facilities for their members.

Residential golf estates have proliferated in the region since the early 1990s, with modern course designs to complement the established old members' layouts. The first was at Dainfern, and the assurance of secure living has since seen many others established between Sandton and Pretoria.

Pretoria Country Club

COURSE DESIGNER Bob Grimsdell
OPENED 1948

Golf has been played on this attractive, leafy site in the wealthy Pretoria suburb of Waterkloof for a hundred years. The club was founded by the German-born philanthropist Sir Julius Jeppe, who owned a shooting lodge on the property. The parkland course has undergone major changes over the years, firstly in the 1940s under Jock Brews and Bob Grimsdell, but none more so than in 2004 when the Gary Player Design team updated it at considerable expense, building new greens and adding an extensive range of deep, steep-faced bunkers.

This upgrade, with bunkers doubled in number to more than ninety, transformed Pretoria Country Club from a gentle members' course into a championship layout that hosts Sunshine Tour events. For all its rich history and tradition, the club had never hosted a national championship until 2006 when the Women's SA Amateur was played there in its centenary year.

The course has two contrasting nines, the front being on the flat side, and the back much more undulating. There is an attractive natural look to the course, with wetlands replacing the old artificial hazards, and native grasses and indigenous trees improving the visual impact.

Pot bunkers add a links flavour to this parkland course, as seen on the par-four 6th (right).
The 8th (above) is a one-shotter to an island green.

Silver Lakes

COURSE DESIGNER Peter Matkovich
OPENED 1993

In keeping with the name of this golf estate, the first of its kind in Pretoria, water is a dominant theme on the course. It comes into play on 11 of the holes, including the final holes on each nine, a par three and par five respectively, where the greens have been built next to each other on an island with palm trees in front of the clubhouse.

Course designer Peter Matkovich has provided exciting risk-and-reward features, and unusual ones at that. The demanding par-four 8th hole has a split fairway separated by a stream. Golfers have a choice of two lines of play. There is a large dam on the back nine, a beautiful feature of the estate, and here Matkovich has again presented options. The par-five 14th has two fairways, one safely to the left of the water, the other on an island in the dam. This alternative route is really only for longer hitters because once your ball is on the island you need to gamble on reaching the green in two across a wide expanse of water.

Silver Lakes is a substantial estate, with some 1 700 homes and a wildlife reserve. Indigenous trees around the course convey the original bushveld look of the property.

Silver Lakes is a modern, risk-and-reward course with plenty of water features, as on the par-four 10th (above) and the par-five 18th (below).

Maccauvlei

COURSE DESIGNERS George Peck/Colonel SV Hotchkin
OPENED 1926

There remains a historic look and timeless feel to Maccauvlei outside the town of Vereeniging, which more than any other contemporary club captures the zeitgeist of golf in South Africa between the two world wars. It was a period in which the club flourished, and its list of members included many leading business and political figures of the day, who travelled by train from Johannesburg to spend weekends at the club's dormy house.

In its secluded setting next to the tree-lined banks of the Vaal River you can turn the clock back on a visit to Maccauvlei, which takes great pride in its heritage. The original clubhouse is unchanged, several rooms having been restored to reflect its grand past. The club might not be as busy as it once was, but continues to ooze grace, charm and character.

Colonel SV Hotchkin, who redesigned the layout back in 1929, called Maccauvlei an 'inland links' because its contours resembled those of a seaside course, with natural sandy bunkers. Hotchkin created the famous par-four 17th, with its massive bunker tumbling back down the fairway from the front of a hidden green. The course hosted four South African Opens, and was restored by Peter Matkovich in the late 1990s.

Maccauvlei is worth the short drive from Johannesburg to the Vaal River for holes like the par-four 6th (above) and the par-three 16th (below).

Gardener Ross

COURSE DESIGNER Ernie Els
OPENED 2007

Expansively wide and super-long golf courses appear to be the modern trend among new designs in Gauteng, typified by this estate layout in the Centurion area. It measures an astounding 7 360 metres from the back tees, with a normal par of 72. Ernie Els, for his second course in South Africa after Oubaai on the Garden Route, has built some of the longest holes in the country. His par-five 13th was officially the longest when opened for play, at 626 metres from the tips. The hole preceding it is a 256-metre par three!

The course rating off the championship tees is a stiff 76, which gives a good idea of its difficulty factor. However, most golfers play Gardener Ross from the club tees, an overall distance of 750 metres shorter, and this is a more enjoyable experience for most. Els and co-designer Greg Letsche have created alternative routes for the higher handicap, and their bunkering is more strategic than penal. The course is similar in look and feel to Oubaai, built in open, virtually treeless countryside with subtle undulations, and with the same design flow to the holes.

Situated near Lanseria Airport, just off the highway between Krugersdorp and Pretoria, Gardener Ross is out in the country and has beautiful vistas of neighbouring hills.

The par-three 17th (above) and the par-four 12th (right) show the expansive design of Gardener Ross, built over rolling Highveld grassland.

Pecanwood

COURSE DESIGNER Jack Nicklaus
OPENED 1998

This pleasant residential golf estate on the rural banks of the Hartbeespoort Dam has generated an attractive new country lifestyle for a growing number of Gauteng city dwellers who have forsaken the hustle and bustle of Sandton, Johannesburg and Pretoria to lead a contented existence behind its secure walls.

Isolated from most conveniences when first opened, Pecanwood has evolved into a busy community with its own school, Pecanwood College, and shopping and business centres next door. It is one of few golf estates that can boast a boat club. With 750 homes, an increasing number of residents are living there permanently, some of them still commuting to work. It is on the edge of the scenic Magaliesberg region, and the mountain range forms a stunning backdrop to the estate. The area is popular as a place to stay, and two other golf estates have since been developed on the banks of Hartbeespoort Dam.

For golfers living at Pecanwood, the bonus is having a superb Jack Nicklaus signature course on which to play, the first from the Golden Bear in this country. Pecanwood is where he introduced South Africans to the concept of a course heavily fortified by bunkers, more than a hundred spread over the 18 holes. The course is on a flat property, once a pecan nut grove (hence the name), and

more than a million cubic metres of soil were brought in so that Nicklaus could do his shaping and provide definition to the topography.

The course may look straightforward and relatively benign with its wide fairways, but the bunkers are frustrating in their ability to lure shots that are not perfectly placed. And then golfers have to deal with the artfully shaped Nicklaus greens, with rounded edges and slopes that lead balls back into bunkers, or the collection areas that are an additional feature of the greens complexes.

Pecanwood might be on the dam, but only one hole is actually on the water's edge, the picturesque par-three 13th where the tee shot needs to carry water all the way to the green. The previous hole, a par five, is just as scenic, Nicklaus having positioned the green so that all you see behind it from the fairway is water, mountains and sky. The course has always enjoyed top-class conditioning.

Pecanwood maintains a high position in South Africa's golf rankings. The par-four 14th (above) and the par-three 13th (right) illustrate the top-notch conditioning and tactical bunkering.

Blair Atholl

COURSE DESIGNER Gary Player
OPENED 2007

Blair Atholl, west of Sandton, was the Gauteng country home of Gary Player for almost twenty-five years before the property was turned into an exclusive golf estate with an 18-hole championship course, where Player pays design homage to Augusta National in Georgia in the United States. His original green jacket, presented at Augusta in 1961 when he won the first of his three Masters, hangs in the opulent Blair Atholl clubhouse.

The course, like Augusta National, is reserved for members and guests. There are other similarities too. The caddies wear white coveralls, and the sight of them walking with a fourball conjures up television images of the Masters. The club has a close relationship with a private Augusta club, Champions Retreat, and their members contest an annual match for the Atlantic Cup.

Augusta is known for elevation changes, and Player has used the undulating terrain at Blair Atholl to create his own. He was helped in this respect by developer Robbie Wray, who acquired not only the grounds of the old Player stud farm, but several neighbouring farms, to create an expansive country living experience that contrasts with urban golf estates. The Crocodile River flows through the course, and comes into play at strategic points.

Player designed a man-sized layout that can adequately handle the extreme distances the modern golf ball travels. From the championship tees it measures 7 536 metres, about 800 metres longer than the average Gauteng course. The club tees at 6 807 metres are the same length as Augusta National is stretched for the Masters. The 16th at Blair Atholl is probably the longest par four in the world at 515 metres off the back, playing uphill.

Several holes at Blair Atholl resemble those at Augusta, like the par-three 3rd, which is enclosed by tall trees, the front of its green having a steep bank above a water hazard. The course ends with an uphill hole, although it is a par five rather than a par four as at Augusta. But Blair Atholl closely approximates Augusta in the sheer width of the course and its strategic bunkering. The fairways are invitingly spacious, and the rough is kept closely trimmed. However, the course does not have two loops of nine, but is routed in a big circular loop for 12 holes before returning to the clubhouse. There is a pretty halfway house built on the banks of the river after the par-three 8th.

Blair Atholl bears a resemblance to Augusta National in the United States, with its large, open bunkers, mature trees and grand scale, as seen on the par-five 18th (left) and 10th (overleaf).

165

Country Club Johannesburg:
WOODMEAD & ROCKLANDS

COURSE DESIGNER Frederick W Hawtree (Woodmead);
Martin Hawtree (Rocklands)
OPENED 1970 (Woodmead); 1992 (Rocklands)

Stature, tradition and a well-heeled membership have never been in short supply at Country Club Johannesburg, but only in recent years has the hierarchical importance of Johannesburg's second oldest golf club been matched by the quality of its golf courses.

Today this club in the northern suburbs has two of the finest layouts in South Africa, comparable to any golfing experience in Gauteng. Known as Woodmead and Rocklands, they are Hawtree family designs, which have benefited substantially from modern makeovers by the Golf Data design and construction company.

Country Club has an unusual history by local golfing standards. It is the only old historic club (founded 1906) that moved to a new site in a modern era of the game. While other older golf clubs around the country had established themselves on existing properties early in the twentieth century, Country Club members played golf on the city outskirts of Johannesburg, in Auckland Park, for more than sixty years before moving to the Khyber Rock area in 1970.

This intelligent, forward-thinking decision by the golfing committee to leave their home club and set up a new 18-hole course in rural farmland paid rich dividends for future generations of members. They acquired enough land that Country Club could build a second course, Rocklands (originally Woodlands), in the early 1990s, with space to spare. Looking at the busy highways and densely populated suburbs surrounding leafy Country Club today, it is hard to imagine the club's beginnings at the dawn of the twentieth century, yet the beauty and solitude of the property, evident once you are inside the gates, still provides a sense of the original isolation, particularly the long drive to the splendid clubhouse.

The par-five 3rd hole on the Woodmead course at Country Club Johannesburg has a narrow entrance to the green, water features and well-placed bunkering.

The Country Club at Auckland Park, still active today, was from its inception a social club. The golf course was short and ordinary and the game was no more important than other sports. The move to Woodmead changed the golfing culture. British designer Fred W Hawtree – at that time the premier architect in Europe – laid out the first course on the undulating terrain, and his son Martin did the second.

Yet the Woodmead layout was not highly regarded until revamped by Golf Data at the turn of the millennium into something longer, more challenging and attractive, with vastly improved fairway bunkering. A palatial new clubhouse was built and kikuyu grass was introduced on the fairways, making an enormous difference to the overall look and playability of the course.

The Woodmead layout uses elevation to great effect throughout its 18 holes to create excellent design variety. There are downhill par fives on the front nine and uphill equivalents at the end of the round. There is a superb trio of holes early in the round – the downhill par-five 3rd, followed by the dramatic-looking par-three 4th, with water guarding the green, and then a first-class long par four through an avenue of pine trees. Gary Player made the first televised hole-in-one in South Africa on the 4th in a Skins Game in the 1980s.

Sunshine Tour professionals have particularly enjoyed the outstanding condition of the course, and its potential for low scoring, since tournaments were first played on the Woodmead in 2005. Marc Cayeux thrilled fans with a closing round of 11-under 61 that year to win the Vodacom Championship. The next year the club started hosting the Telkom PGA Championship, and in 2008 Louis Oosthuizen posted a 28-under-par total of 260, one shy of equalling the all-time Sunshine Tour record.

Woodmead is a parkland layout, heavily treed in places, contrasting with the more open Highveld look of Rocklands, with its indigenous trees and rocky outcrops. The revamp of Rocklands was completed in 2009, and at 7 000 metres in length it no longer stands in Woodmead's shadow.

Woodmead's par-four 17th (above) has sunk many tournament dreams. Rockland's par-three 15th (below) depicts the more open, grassland finishes that differentiate it from Woodmead. The dogleg par-four 5th at Rocklands (overleaf) requires a downhill approach shot over water.

River Club

COURSE DESIGNER Bob Grimsdell
OPENED 1968

This private, members-only course in Sandton is a stunning parkland jewel next to the Jukskei River, on undulating terrain that has helped create a rich variety of golfing holes. Although exclusive, with a relatively small membership, it is an unpretentious club, where the enjoyment of golf takes precedence. The clubhouse is smaller than most Sandton homes.

The club was created by the late industrialist Charles Sydney 'Punch' Barlow to accommodate discerning (and wealthy) golfers who wanted a golf club where they could turn up at any time and arrange a game without the fuss of booking times in advance. Its members are mainly business leaders.

The original Bob Grimsdell layout was upgraded in the late 1990s by club manager Roy Yates, working with designer Rob O'Friel, and their changes brought a dramatic improvement. Yates introduced magnificent standards of conditioning, which are now synonymous with golf at the River Club.

The course is not long by Gauteng standards, but the sloping lie of the land and famously fast greens make for challenging golf nevertheless. The last five holes, starting with the par-three 14th on the banks of the river, would rate among the best finishing stretches in South Africa.

First-rate conditioning is evident on the par-four 7th (above) and the par-four 12th (right). The par-four 3rd (overleaf) has a slightly raised green, making it a small target.

Royal Johannesburg & Kensington:
EAST & WEST

COURSE DESIGNERS Laurie Waters (West); Bob Grimsdell (East)
OPENED 1910 (West); 1935 (East)

When playing golf at Royal's two magnificent parkland layouts today, with their tree-lined fairways, it is hard to imagine that the original golf course on this property a century ago was designed to replicate the Old Course at St Andrews in Scotland.

When the Johannesburg Golf Club (founded 1890) moved to this barren Orange Grove site in 1910 the club professional was Laurie Waters, who was entrusted with the design of the 18-hole course. Waters hailed from St Andrews, where he had been an apprentice under Old Tom Morris in the 1890s. His 'links' at Orange Grove followed a similar anti-clockwise routing to the Old Course, and had its own 'loop' of three holes at the far end before returning to the clubhouse. He built a wide variety of bunkers in the Scottish tradition, including what was described as 'many vicious small pot bunkers'. At 5 490 metres, it was a fierce test for that time, with a bogey (par) of 79.

It was a pioneering course for the then Transvaal, and it was the first course in the province to have grass greens, the Florida strain that was to be so successful on the Highveld. Waters's design formed the foundation of Royal's West course as we know it today. He must have felt at home on this layout, and in 1920 he not surprisingly won the first South African Open played there.

The early club professionals at Royal (the club received its royal charter in 1931) had a considerable influence on the future progress of the club. Waters left in 1920, to be replaced by George Peck (another who dabbled in course design). In 1926 he was succeeded by the man regarded as the father of modern South African golf course architecture, Bob Grimsdell.

Grimsdell had emigrated here from England as a teenager, served with the South African forces in France during the First World War, and his first job as a club pro was at Chorley in Lancashire. He showed an early interest in golf

Stately old poplars line many fairways of Royal Johannesburg's two courses, as on the par-four 3rd hole of the East course.

179

course design, and met the famous British course architect Harry Colt before returning to Cape Town, where he was employed at Mowbray Golf Club.

Grimsdell's first design opportunity was on the West course, from 1929 onwards, implementing changes suggested by Colonel SV Hotchkin, who was touring the country following his work at Humewood. Four years later Royal decided the course had become so congested that another 18 holes were necessary. Adjoining farmland was bought, and work started in 1933 on what was to become Grimsdell's design masterpiece, the East course. It took him two years to complete, such was the enormous task of clearing the land by hand with no earthmoving machinery. Grass for the fairways came from the lawns of members' homes. He built 21 new holes, 7 for the old course and 14 for the new, and that is what they were called, the Old and New. But the opening of the current clubhouse in 1939 meant that the routing of the courses had to be changed. From then on they were known as East and West.

The East has been Royal's championship course ever since, staging seven SA Opens between 1946 and 1986 (the last one held there) and five SA Amateurs, the last of those in 1991. It hosted two Commonwealth amateur tournaments, the men's in 1959 and the women's in 2007. South Africa won the men's event with a team that included three Royal members, Reg Taylor, Jannie le Roux and Arthur Walker. The visiting nations were effusive in their praise of the East, calling it 'one of the best inland courses in the world'. Today the club stages the Joburg Open on the European Tour, using both courses.

Royal long held the image of an old-fashioned, traditional golf club, pervaded by an old-school-tie atmosphere, but more than a hundred years of history went by the wayside after a historic merger with Kensington Golf Club in 1998. Royal was struggling financially and had a dwindling and ageing membership, while Kensington was selling off its course for a property development. It made sense to join forces, even though the members of the two clubs were socially poles apart. The money from Kensington paid for Golf Data to do a major upgrade of the two Royal courses, including a handful of new holes on both the West and East. Today the new club has a vibrant unified membership.

The two courses complement each other perfectly. The East is long and demanding (just under 7 000 metres with some extremely strong par fours), a superb challenge for the low handicaps at the club. The West is a shorter, easier but nevertheless testing experience. In fact, the West has closed the gap on the East in terms of shot making, and is far from the pushover it once was, although it is still an under-rated layout.

A stream adds to the shot-making required on the East course's par-five 6th (above) and the West course's par-four 11th (below). The par-four 3rd on the West course (overleaf) requires a draw off the tee and a long approach.

Glendower

COURSE DESIGNER Charles Hugh Alison
OPENED 1937

This Johannesburg course is one of South Africa's great championship layouts, but one which curiously has not been used for that purpose since the historic 1997 South African Open. However, having been extensively modernised and improved by Golf Data in 2008/09, and with the refurbishment of its clubhouse, Glendower should not be overlooked much longer.

Glendower and the nearby East course at Royal Johannesburg & Kensington have always stood comparison as the two most challenging experiences in Gauteng, and their histories are closely intertwined. Both were built in the depression years of the 1930s, designed by men – Charles Alison and Bob Grimsdell – with links to the famous British architect Harry Colt. Alison was a partner of Colt's who retired to South Africa and was responsible for both Glendower and Bryanston, another championship quality layout.

Early tournaments at Glendower and Royal East were handsomely won by Bobby Locke, who in 1939 set a world record at Glendower with rounds of 66-69-66-64 for a score of 265. He won that Transvaal Open by 26 shots.

Yet Glendower played second fiddle in social standing and influence to Royal, and it was not until the club celebrated its fiftieth anniversary in 1987 that it was awarded its first South African championship, the Amateur, where Ben Fouchee remarkably won all three of the trophies.

From that introduction there followed three SA Opens at Glendower in the space of eight years, none more significant than the one in 1997 when Vijay Singh became the first champion of colour, in the first year the Open became part of the European Tour. Singh overcame a stellar South African lineup, chased home by Nick Price, Ernie Els, Mark McNulty, Fulton Allem and Retief Goosen, in that order.

Glendower greets you with a succession of strong holes, and shares another link with Royal East as well as with Durban Country Club in having a par-four, par-three and par-five in the opening three holes. The par-five 2nd at Glendower, with its tee shot over a dam to a lower fairway, bordered by a stream on the left and trees on the right, was chosen by Locke in his list of great holes.

Golf Data designer Sean Quinn has in his redesign at Glendower opened up water vistas next to the green of the intimidating par-four 10th and created new green sites for the 5th and 18th, yet retained the essential vision of the layout.

The par-four 7th hole shows why Glendower is one of the Highveld's championship courses.

Every hole is a great hole at Glendower, requiring precision from tee to green. Clockwise from top left: the par-four 11th calls for a fade off the tee, while the par-four 10th and par-five 2nd demand caution to avoid the water and reach the green.

Ebotse

COURSE DESIGNER Peter Matkovich
OPENED 2008

When golf course architect Peter Matkovich first saw the colossal sand hills on the site of a disused quarry in Benoni where he was meant to build Ebotse, he made a decision that was to save the developers a big chunk of their projected budget. Instead of removing the sand at great expense, he used it to create what is known in golf course architecture as a dirt-pile design.

The sand was dispersed and shaped into uneven, flowing mounds between holes, giving a links-like character to what would have been a flat, uninteresting piece of land next to Rynfield Lake. It is not a deliberate attempt to build an artificial links by adding dirt, as Gary Player did at The Links at Fancourt; instead, the mounds lend distinctive character to each hole, and the result is a uniquely rugged golf course for Gauteng, in contrast to the pretty parkland layouts that are typical of the region.

The Ebotse course is not all high dunes, but has a rumpled and distressed look, with jagged mounds and steep slopes adding definition to the terrain. It is a course of contrasts and elevation changes. You begin each nine with stunning links-type holes running between the dunes, and play the finishing holes, the 9th and 18th, alongside the lake that is a feature of the estate.

The Ebotse estate is a success story from an environmental angle. The developers have restored a large wetlands area at one end of the lake that was previously used by off-road bike and 4x4 enthusiasts, but is now attracting plentiful birdlife.

While the course is dramatic and challenging to play, a big talking point for visitors to Ebotse is the practice range facility, a large expanse of water in a canyon-like amphitheatre surrounded by high dunes and golf holes. Floating balls are used, and the aiming points for golfers are rowing boats out in the dam. The balls are collected after they have drifted back to shore.

Opposite the range is a high slope on top of which houses have been built, and below that is the par-five 12th, running along the edge of the lake. Ebotse is not long, but it is tight, and accuracy off the tee is key to scoring well.

Ebotse breaks the mould of Highveld parkland courses, offering a unique dirt-pile design with Irish links elements, as seen in the par-three 8th hole (above) and the par-four 10th (right).

South Africa's best golf holes

This list of 'best holes' in South Africa is a fun look at individual holes rather than a course as a whole. There are many different methods of judging a course or hole and the list below is in no way definitive or mathematically calculated. Instead, it includes the holes that immediately came to mind when the author and photographer discussed 'a great short par four' or 'an excellent risk-and-reward par five'. South Africa has so many fantastic courses and hundreds of great holes that are worthy of inclusion that the difficulty was to keep the list short. This section on spectacular holes really brings into focus the impressive number of incredible courses South Africa has. Each golfer probably has his or her own list of best holes, and perhaps this one will make you think about yours.

MOST SPECTACULAR HOLES (18)
Arabella 8th par five
Champagne Sports 4th par three
Durban CC 2nd par three
Fish River Sun 12th par five
Gary Player CC 9th par five
Goose Valley 11th par three
Hans Merensky 8th par three
Leopard Creek 13th par five
Lost City 13th par three
Milnerton 2nd par four
Oubaai 17th par three
Pezula 13th par five
Pinnacle Point 7th par three
Prince's Grant 15th par five
Simola 2nd par four
Sishen 6th par five
Umdoni Park 18th par five
Wild Coast Sun 13th par three

BEST SHORT PAR THREES (8)
Beachwood 2nd
Cotswold Downs 5th
Goose Valley 11th
Humewood 6th
Pinnacle Point 7th
Royal Johannesburg: West 5th
San Lameer 4th
Southbroom 4th

BEST MEDIUM PAR THREES (8)
Arabella 17th
Atlantic Beach 12th
Blair Atholl 3rd
Durban CC 2nd
East London 17th
Hans Merensky 8th
Lost City 15th
Fancourt Montagu 17th

BEST LONG PAR THREES (8)
George 17th
Leopard Creek 16th
Oubaai 6th
River Club 17th
Royal Johannesburg: East 2nd
Simola 6th
The Links at Fancourt 2nd
Zebula CC 17th

BEST PAR FOURS (12)
Blair Atholl 4th
Glendower 7th
Humewood 13th
Lost City 9th
Fancourt Montagu 7th
Prince's Grant 2nd
River Club 16th
Royal Cape 14th
Royal Johannesburg: East 11th
Sishen 7th
Woodmead 17th
Zimbali 18th

BEST SHORT PAR FOURS (16)
Arabella 16th
Champagne Sports 10th
Clovelly 14th
De Zalze 18th
Durban CC 18th
East London 9th
Ebotse 10th
Elements 6th
Fancourt Outeniqua 5th
Gary Player CC 9th
Pearl Valley 17th
Pezula 14th
Pinnacle Point 8th
St Francis Links 5th
The Links at Fancourt 14th
Victoria CC 16th

BEST PAR FIVES (8)
Cotswold Downs 1st
Durban CC 3rd
East London 3rd
Glendower 2nd
Pinnacle Point 5th
Prince's Grant 15th
Stellenbosch 14th
The Links at Fancourt 9th

BEST GAMBLING PAR FIVES (8)
Clovelly 15th
Elements 18th
Gary Player CC 9th
Leopard Creek 18th
Fancourt Outeniqua 17th
Pearl Valley 13th
Silver Lakes 14th
Steenberg 18th

Creative design

Bob Grimsdell

Gary Player

Jack Nicklaus

Peter Matkovich

The four most influential golf course architects in South Africa have been Bob Grimsdell, Gary Player, Peter Matkovich and, more recently, Jack Nicklaus. They are responsible for designing at least a third of South Africa's 18-hole courses, the majority constituting some of the best layouts we play on today.

All four have links to golf other than through design. Player and Nicklaus are golfing legends; Grimsdell was a fine golfer in his youth – runner-up in the 1931 South African Open – as was Matkovich, who at one time caddied for Player. Both Grimsdell and Matkovich were club pros, and entered design through working on their club's courses, Grimsdell at Royal Johannesburg and Matkovich at Umhlali Country Club.

The pioneer was Grimsdell, who designed a multitude of courses from 1929 to 1979. He made it a full-time profession after the Second World War, when the game was exploding and new golf clubs were springing up everywhere.

His original designs can be found in every major centre, but where Grimsdell left a legacy was in the many courses he built in the platteland, and which helped grow the game among the Afrikaans community. He has courses in places as diverse as Sishen, Phalaborwa, Ellisras, Orkney, Kimberley, Nelspruit, Welkom and Mossel Bay.

Like the early designers in the United States, Grimsdell travelled far and wide, and also redesigned many layouts. He was a master at routing courses, a skill he gained while sorting out the East and West courses at Royal Johannesburg, and creating a balance and rhythm to the holes. But he did not leave us with any kind of signature that put a stamp on his work. His greens tended to be flat and plain in shape, and the strength of his old courses was rather in the excellent routing and design variety of the layouts.

Player dabbled in golf course design from the early 1970s onwards, and his first major undertaking was the Gary Player Country Club at Sun City with Ron Kirby, an early partner. Although that course is still regarded as among his best, his finest creative work is The Links at Fancourt, a remarkable concept for South Africa. The Player name and reputation enabled him to procure some of the best commissions in the estate boom that began in the 1990s, notably Fancourt, Leopard Creek and Blair Atholl. Much of this work was done with the assistance of Phil Jacobs.

Matkovich's breakthrough came in the early 1990s with San Lameer. He has been a prolific designer ever since, excelling with his bold, innovative ideas, and is in demand for his ability to turn the most unattractive of sites into courses that golfers have come to enjoy. His courses have unusual features, and he loves to surprise golfers with scary, risk-and-reward holes. His spectacular cliffside design at Pinnacle Point captured worldwide attention, and he went beyond conventional thinking with his par-60 course at Simbithi. He has also designed courses in Zimbabwe and Mauritius.

Nicklaus received his first South African commission in the mid-1990s when he was approached to design Simola, and he has had regular contracts since, bringing his own flawless style of design here, particularly the dramatic use of bunkering to define holes and provide character to a course. Although his fee is high, the power of the Nicklaus name to sell an estate has paid dividends for developers. The Golden Bear's approach to design influenced the thinking of Ernie Els, who took on Greg Letsche, a former Nicklaus employee, as his right-hand man, and also the Golf Data design company that has built all his layouts.

ACKNOWLEDGEMENTS

There are two individuals that have particularly steered my photography career to date. Firstly, Malcolm Funston's wildlife photography and books encouraged me to take photography more seriously. More recently, Grant Leversha's images inspired me to attempt to similarly capture the beauty and elegance of golf courses.

My thanks go to the editors of two golf magazines in South Africa who have supported me over the years and created a number of opportunities, namely Stuart McLean of *Golf Digest South Africa* and Brandon de Kock of *Compleat Golfer*. I was thrilled that Stuart agreed to write the accompanying text for this book, and I could not think of a better creative partner. Brandon, among other things, laid the foundation of my association with Peter Matkovich and Andy Bean of Matkovich & Hayes Golf Estate Solutions, which has developed into a wonderful relationship.

Further gratitude goes to my great friend, professional photographer Neil Kirby. Thanks for all your help on the technical side of photography, your tips on equipment and especially the guidance you provided in crossing the digital divide.

On the greens, a big thank you to all the club CEOs, managers, golf directors and course superintendents who gave me access to their courses and who went out of their way to assist me.

To all my friends with whom I have played and enjoyed the fantastic game of golf – thank you. To my parents, thank you for all the opportunities offered as well as the encouragement and support you have given through all my endeavours.

Finally, doing what I do requires a lot of travel and time spent away from home, so my heartfelt thanks are for my wife, Kerese, for all her advice, support and love along the way.

First published in 2009 by Struik Travel & Heritage
(an imprint of Random House Struik (Pty) Ltd)
Company Reg. No. 1966/003153/07
80 McKenzie Street, Cape Town, 8001
PO Box 1144, Cape Town, 8000, South Africa

www.randomstruik.co.za

Copyright © in published edition: Random House Struik 2009
Copyright © in text and captions: Stuart McLean (text) and Jamie Thom (captions) 2009
Copyright © in photographs: Jamie Thom 2009, with the exception of those credited opposite
Copyright © in maps: Random House Struik 2009

Publisher: Claudia Dos Santos
Managing editor: Roelien Theron
Project co-ordinator: Alana Bolligelo
Editor: Roxanne Reid
Designer and cartographer: Catherine Coetzer
Proofreader: Joy Clack

Reproduction by Hirt & Carter Cape (Pty) Ltd
Printed and bound by Kyodo Nation Printing Services Co., Ltd

ISBN 978 1 77007 622 8

10 9 8 7 6 5 4 3 2 1

Front cover: Erinvale, par-three 8th hole
Half-title page: St Francis Links, par-three 4th hole
Title page: Leopard Creek, par-five 13th hole
Back cover: Sishen, par-four 7th hole

Photographic credits
Pages 11 (left and centre) Shaen Adey/IOA, (right) Lanz von Hörsten/IOA; 39 (left) Walter Knirr/IOA, (centre) Mark Skinner/IOA, (right) Lanz von Hörsten/IOA; 73 (left) Hein von Hörsten/IOA, (centre) Peter Pickford/IOA, (right) Walter Knirr/IOA; 93 (left) Shaen Adey/IOA, (centre) Walter Knirr/IOA, (right) Nigel Dennis/IOA; 155 (left and right) Walter Knirr/IOA, (centre) Hein von Hörsten/IOA; 191 (golf designers); 191 (left) Courtesy of the Royal Johannesburg & Kensington Golf Club
IOA = Images of Africa

Over 50 000 unique African images available to purchase from our image bank at:
www.imagesofafrica.co.za

For more information about Jamie Thom's photography see:
www.golfart.co.za and www.jamiethom.com

All rights reserved. No part of this publication may be reproduced, stored in a retrieval system or transmitted, in any form or by any means, electronic, mechanical, photocopying, recording or otherwise, without the prior written permission of the publishers and the copyright holder(s).